The Book
of Tulips

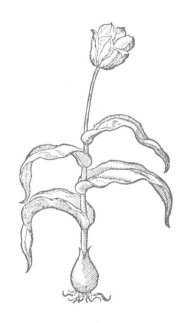

frontispiece: Generations of painters have
been inspired by the tulip's beauty. This
magnificent example is by Hans Bollongier
(1600–45).

Tom Lodewijk

The Book of Tulips

Edited by Ruth Buchan

The Vendome Press
New York   Paris   Lausanne
Distributed by The Viking Press

For Mary Lasker
and Enid Haupt

*Tulipa Remmerlandi Elegan
fondo alba oriz purpuriœ
rubent: arnata .*

Acknowledgments
The publisher would like particularly to thank the late J.A. Janse,
for his assistance in obtaining illustrations and technical information,
and T. Hoog of Bennebroek as well as J.F. Ch. Dix of Heemstede,
for making available unpublished manuscripts.
The Dutch Bulb Center at Hillegom supplied many illustrations
and other technical information and has made a major contribution
toward the publication of this book, as have the librarian
of the Royal Dutch Bulb Society, the director of the Frans Hals Museum
in Haarlem, the Teylers Foundation of Haarlem, and the directors
of the Keukenhof National Flower Park in Lisse.
Finally, but most important, we acknowledge a debt of gratitude
to the directors of the L. Stassen Jr., Co. in Hillegom,
which provided reproductions of the paintings of the late H. Rol.

Picture research: Leo Verbeek
Layout: Pieter van Delft and Jack Botermans, ADM International, Amsterdam
Typographical design: Marlene Rothkin Vine
Translation from the Dutch: Stephen T. Moskey
Photolithography: R.C.O., Velp, The Netherlands

Distributed 1979 in the United States of America
by The Viking Press, 625 Madison Avenue, New York, N.Y. 10022
Distributed in Canada by Penguin Books Canada Limited

Library of Congress Catalog Card Number: 79–5093
ISBN: 0–670–18063–7
Printed and bound in Italy by GEA, Milan.

One of the most beautiful tulips ever
produced was the Admiral, developed by
the Bailiff of Kennemerland in the early
17th century. Its exquisite shape and color
earned it recognition as the apex of the
horticulturist's craft in those days.

Contents

Gras-Maendt, or "grass month," the Old Dutch name for the month of April, is pictured here in a print from the book *De verstandige Huyshoulder* ("The Wise Homeowner"), which dates from 1669. Spring is personified by the goddess Venus who is presented with a flower, the tulip, which was then the most expensive and exclusive flower of Dutch society. The tulip still holds a unique position in The Netherlands, even if due only to the Keukenhof Park, pictured below.

Aprillis /   Gras-Maendt.

Introduction

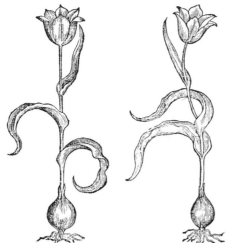

Once upon a time there was a Persian youth named Farhad who was enamored of a beautiful girl, Shirin. We do not know whether it was through malice or whether it was the result of a human error, but rumor reached him that his beloved had been killed. Farhad mounted his favorite horse and galloped full speed straight off the edge of a rocky escarpment, meeting death instantly. As the blood seeped out of his many wounds, bright red tulips sprang up all around. And that is why the red tulip now represents a declaration of love in the language of flowers. In Persia it was the emblem of perfect love, and if offered by a young man to his beloved, he was saying: "As the redness of this flower, I am on fire with love, and as the blackness of its center, my heart is burnt to a coal."

In the book *Birthday Gems*, an offshoot of *The Language of Flowers* (1836), there are two spring days with tulips designated as the birthday flower. March 21 is represented by the purple tulip, and in this context it signifies undying love. May 17 has the yellow tulip for its flower, and its meaning is given here as hopeless love. The little volume assures us, however, that in the language of flowers, the meaning may be changed from cruel to kind by presenting the flower upside down.

Yet rich as morn of many hue
When flashing clouds through darkness strike,
The tulip's petals shine in dew
All beautiful, yet none alike.

Montgomery

right: Madame de Pompadour (1721–64), the favorite of Louis XV of France, was a great admirer of flowers. Haarlem florists supplied flowers to the French court in great quantities and at very great expense. These flowers were used not only for decorating the great halls of palaces, but also for the attire of ladies who wished to trim their plunging necklines with such costly blossoms as tulips and hyacinths.

below: As part of the celebration of her silver wedding anniversary in 1962, Her Majesty Queen Juliana of The Netherlands treated her guests to a visit to Keukenhof Park. This photograph, taken during that visit, shows the Empress Farah Diba of Iran in the front left corner. Her husband, Shah Reza Mohammed Pahlavi, is just behind her, engaged in conversation with Prince Philip of England.

1 Tulips Everywhere

In the early part of the 20th century, a session with a photographer meant dressing up in one's Sunday best and, once in his studio, standing absolutely motionless to avoid blurring the negative. This photograph, taken at a bulb nursery in Kennemerland more than 70 years ago, tells us something about those times. Here, a clear distinction is made between gentlemen and simple, working folk; in the background, fieldhands with the tools of their trade stand as if stopping momentarily from their labors while owners looking prosperous and self-assured pose in the foreground.

During the reign of the Sun King, Louis XIV of France (1638–1715), it became the fashion for ladies of society and the Court to adorn themselves, rather than their boudoirs, with the costliest tulip blossoms they could find. The style of the gowns in that era—and much admired it was—presented the ladies with an unequaled receptacle—the deep décolletage—for these showy blossoms. The tulips, only recently introduced to Europe from the great palaces of the East, were the most exotic as well as the most expensive ornaments to be had. And, thus, they earned their right of place.

Of course, the choice of variety was important. Some tulips were inexpensive, but the range in cost was as great as that of color and shape. One could pay as much for a rare bulb as for a country estate, and *that* made the tulip the flower to flaunt on the bosom.

Times have changed, though. The flower that only a hundred years ago was an upper-class status symbol has, since the early part of the 20th century, come within everyone's reach. The tulip is to be seen everywhere, both as a living plant and as a decorative motif. Artisans and craftsmen draw on the tulip's form for inspiration and imitation. Wrought iron railings, porcelain (see pages 20–22), glassware (see page 20), earthenware, needlework (see page 29), fashion, sculpture, furniture (see page 29), tiles (see pages 13–15, 22), and painting (see pages 2, 19, 56, 57) have all at one time or another incorporated or reproduced the tulip's graceful proportions.

Rubens painted a picture of his wife in her tulip garden, and such artists as Breughel, van Huysam, and Elliger produced beautiful

right: Exhibitions have been largely responsible for spreading the popularity of the tulip. The 1865 International Garden Show held in the Amsterdam Hall of Industry, shown here in a contemporary engraving, included a large, stunning entry by bulb growers.

below: Tulips are interwoven with a tree of life in the fine example of Frisian penmanship in this letter dated 1766. The letter opens with the line: "May I enjoy your company as long as the Good Lord grants us time together. . ." Throughout time, the tulip has variously symbolized love, life, and death.

studies of flower arrangements. Beverly Nichols in *The Art of Flower Arrangement* says that *A Vase of Flowers in a Window* by Ambrosius Bosschaert, which is made up of splendid tulips, "must be regarded as one of the supreme flower paintings of all time."

The design was also a favorite in textiles, appearing in tapestries and printed fabrics throughout Europe in the 18th and 19th centuries. Today some of the latest designs for linens feature cheerful tulip patterns, and we find new crystal, or reproductions of old crystal, being etched with a tulip design. Thus, the flower whose design so intrigued the artists and artisans of centuries ago continues to hold its place in the decorative arts of today's world.

The Tulip in Literature

The tulip also has a place in literature. The famous French writer Alexandre Dumas père (1802–70) turned to the tulip for thematic inspiration in his celebrated novel *The Black Tulip*. The book is entirely the product of his imagination. No black tulip existed at the time the novel was written, and it is filled with frivolous historical inaccuracies: the tulip was supposedly brought to Holland from Ceylon by the Portuguese. His explanation of how the tulip grows (plant the bulb in a pot in April and it blooms in a few days) is ludicrous, as is his explanation of how one makes a black tulip (spray the bulb with black dye and put it in a dark spot). But the story was

left: A jubilee of colors, such as that seen here wrapped in the grey tissue paper used by florists and flower merchants throughout The Netherlands, is a common sight in many countries of the world. By speeding up or delaying the blooming process, tulips can be "scheduled" for delivery at appropriate times of the year.

right: In Holland, it would be a gross social blunder to present your hostess or mother on her birthday with less than ten tulips. This is one of those strange, unwritten rules of etiquette that must be strictly observed. In other countries of the world, though, one, two, or even three carefully chosen tulips may be considered a proper gift.

popular then and is still read today. Fact caught up with fiction, and a black tulip was later developed and was called 'La Tulipe Noire.'

Another Frenchman, Jacques Norman, was the author of a successful comedy in verse, *L'Amiral*, inspired by the 'Admiral Liekens' tulip that was sold for more than $20,000. Love, triumph, and tulipomania are the themes of this work. The playwright places the action in 1795 to coincide with the French occupation of Holland, even though the tulip craze actually occurred a hundred years before that.

The Frenchman Miguel Zamaçois was also inspired by the tulip to write a play in verse, *La Fleur Merveilleuse*. But rather than rely on his imagination for material, he actually traveled to Haarlem to savor some of Holland's local color. He was by profession a painter who had studied under the artist Gérôme. Gérôme had painted a still-enigmatic work entitled *Folie Tulipienne*, which, it is thought, inspired Zamaçois to write his play.

La Fleur Merveilleuse was performed in Paris by the Comédie Française with lavishly decorated sets portraying the Grote Markt in Haarlem and bulb fields in full bloom. There were, however, no bulb fields in Holland in the 18th century.

No Dutch author has written a play in which the tulip or tulipomania are central themes; however, Zamaçois' play was translated into Dutch by J. Baarslag and performed by The Netherlands Drama Company in the early 1900s. The French version was again revived in 1922 at the Odéon Theatre in Paris and ran successfully there for some time.

These baskets from the 1920s were used to display profuse bouquets of bulb flowers.

Holland's commercial enterprises created the need for depiction of bulb flowers that could be used in promoting Dutch bulbs. The Haarlem film maker, J. C. Mol, for example, was commissioned by the Central Bulb Association to produce the popular film *From Bulb to Bloom*. And while Dutch literary achievement in this area has been slim, artistic output has been tremendous.

The Bulb District: de Bollenstreek

Although there may be enormous interest in the tulip as an element of design, or as an inspiration in other art forms, love for the tulip in its living form is even greater. The crowds of tourists from all over the world who each year pour into Holland's Keukenhof Park (see page 7), her bulb fields, and flower shows testify to this flower's devoted following. Even the name of the bulb-growing region, de Bollenstreek ("bulb district"), comes from the chief product of the area.

While there may be many areas of the world where bulbs are grown, there is only one Bollenstreek—that region between Haarlem and Leiden in the western part of The Netherlands where the Dutch bulb industry has chosen to concentrate itself, a relatively small "corridor" with dunes to the west and dairy farms to the east. All bulb-related activities are carried out here: auctions, wholesale markets, export companies, tulip and bulb growers' associations, information bureaus, and research and development institutes. This is the true heart of the industry.

right: Tulip motifs were used in the 17th century to decorate glazed tiles. Tiles were often designed so that two of them could be placed together to form a larger pattern, as shown here.

left: This stone plaque, dated 1755, once graced the façade of a house that in 1636, at the height of the tulipomania, sold for three tulip bulbs. A later owner of that house put up the plaque. At the time of the tulipomania, or "wind trade" as it is sometimes called, innkeepers often called their establishments "The Three Tulip Bulbs"; after the collapse of the wind trade in 1637, many changed the word "tulip" to "silly."

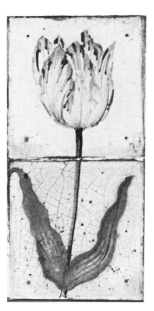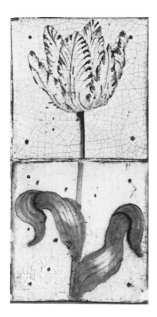

Those who wish to experience the magnificent view of field after field of vibrant color (see page 23) have only a very few weeks of the year to do so. Once the flowers are gone, there is little of interest in the region. The flat, gray acres are accented only by the red roof tiles of farmhouses and bulb sheds. Ditches and roads crisscross the landscape, bordered now and then by rows of houses, greenhouses, and storage buildings (see pages 70, 71).

Long ago the dunes actually extended to (and sometimes crossed) the Heereweg—what is now the main road between Haarlem and Leiden (see page 44). The dunes were a hunter's and trapper's paradise. Old chronicles refer to the area as the "Wilderness of Holland," and even the Roman emperor Claudius spoke of the merciless wilds through which his armies had to pass. .

Around 860 A.D. the mouth of the Rhine, then located near Katwijk, had filled with silt to such an extent that it actually was closed off. As a result, a network of marshes and small lakes was formed around the town of Sassenheim, which today is famous for boating, fishing, and other water sports. The Haarlemermeer ("Lake Haarlem"), a large body of water to the east of the region, was often subjected to violent storms that raised the water level of the lake and eroded the dunes, which were gradually pushed back. The sandy soil that remained now serves as the perfect medium for growing bulbs (see page 71).

The bulb region was the first area of the Low Countries to be visited by Christian missionaries, and it was there in Foreholte (now

below: These 16th-century flowered tiles were found in a building in Anatolia in southern Turkey. They are made of two layers of clay and a grey base with a pure white surface. These are predecessors of Dutch tiles with flower motifs. They illustrate the Turkish artist's idealization of the flower shown here: pointed, arching petals and a striped color pattern.

14

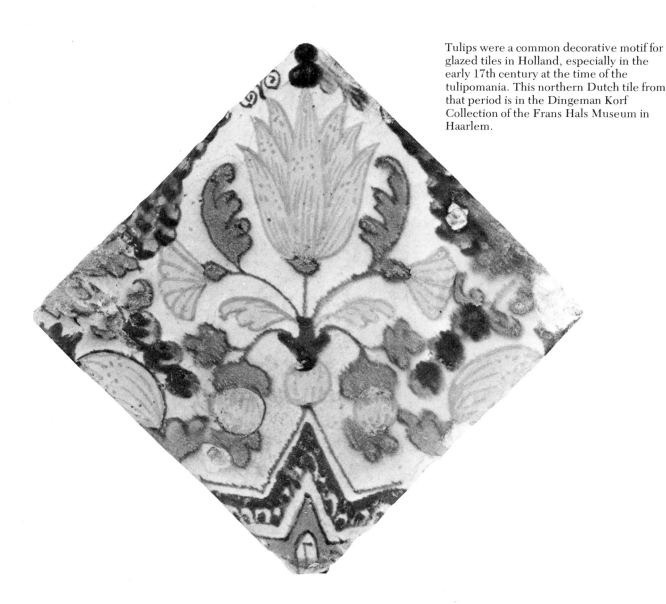

Tulips were a common decorative motif for glazed tiles in Holland, especially in the early 17th century at the time of the tulipomania. This northern Dutch tile from that period is in the Dingeman Korf Collection of the Frans Hals Museum in Haarlem.

Voorhout) that the Benedictine monk Adalbertus first established Christianity in The Netherlands.

The people native to this region were fisherman, farmers, and trappers of small animals. They suffered through invasion, occupation, and plundering carried on by a succession of foreigners: Norsemen, Danes, and, much later, troops and mercenaries of the Spanish Duke Albrecht, who became Governor-General of Holland in 1596.

But in the early 17th century, the Twelve-Year Truce with Spain ushered in an era of peace and prosperity—the Golden Century. The Heereweg increased in importance as the only road between the commercial capital in Amsterdam and the center of government in The Hague. Men who controlled the affairs of state as well as their own business interests often traveled the Heereweg between these two cities. When they stopped at the Old Scholar Tavern in Bennebroek or the White Swan Inn near Lisse to refresh themselves during the long journey, their eyes would fall upon the romantic landscape cradled between the dunes and the lake. They found it so pleasing that they began to build their summer houses in De Gooi, near the old battle fields, and in the "Wilderness of Holland." Great houses and castles with extensive pleasure gardens soon graced the gentle countryside.

However, the good life came to an abrupt end two hundred years later. Napoleon invaded Holland in 1805 and treated it as he valued it: the "delta of French rivers." The once busy quays in Dutch ports were stilled, and the economic life of Holland came to a halt. The country stagnated for ten years.

below: The Double tulip was not generally popular during the 17th century. It was not until the mid-18th century that it was considered worthy of mention in plant books. However, Double tulips reproduced here are from the *Herboricum* of the Bavarian pharmacist Basilius Besler (1561–1627), published in 1613 in two volumes, which depicted 660 tulip varieties in 374 engravings.

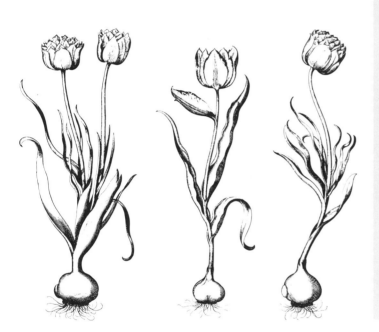

N O T I T I E

Van Nombers, Namen en Gewichten van

T U L P E N,

Die op Woenſdag den 16. Mey 1708.

Sullen verkocht werden in den Tuyn van

H E N R I C U S van der H E Y M,

'*t Eerſte Bed.*

No.		Aſen.	
1.	{ Sultaan.		
	{ Bagt. Potteau.	260.	9
2.	Bagt. Queva. 1696.	930.	22
3.	{ Bagt. Superbe.	930.	
	{ Policionel.		11
4.	{ Archeduc.		
	{ Bifar Proferpine oude.	480.	5
5.	Bagt. Koning van Zweden.	1100.	52 –
6.	{ Nouvelle de St. Omer.	400.	3 .
	{ Archeduc.		
7.	{ Triumph d' Europe.		14
	{ Bagt. No. 2. Potteau.	560.	
8.	Bagt. Lancie.	860.	19
9.	{ Bagt. Buiſſon Ardant.	950.	39
	{ Gran Doge.		
10.	{ Policionel.		. 20
	{ Bagt. Racine d' Angletterre.	910.	
11.	Bagt. bruine de Triſtran.	1120.	151
12.	{ Bagt. No. 2. 1696. -- --	330.	25
	{ Triumph d' Europe.		
			370

When Holland was finally liberated from the French in 1815 this did not mean an immediate return to the prosperity of earlier days. The magnificent country mansions, which had fallen into disrepair, were demolished and later replaced by the ugly row houses of the industrial revolution. Today only the names of these once stately residences remain as place names: Bronkhorst, Klinkenberg, Neerenburg, Elsbroek, Meer en Dorp, and Broekhorst.

One thing, though, had not been changed: the erosion of the dunes continued. In the latter half of the 19th century and the early part of the 20th century the need for sand for the construction of workers' housing ate away at the already fragile dunes. Post coaches no longer rode the Heereweg; they had been replaced by a steam-powered train named the "Bello" that now was responsible for carrying passengers between Amsterdam and Rotterdam.

Keukenhof: the Tulip Paradise

The bulb industry began to expand during the early years of the 20th century. Improvements in transportation meant that people could visit the region. At first, only the slow steam engine pulling long trains brought tourists to the area. Later, bicycles and automobiles brought them, creating traffic jams that today have become so bad that they dampen one's enthusiasm for a visit to the fields.

Everyone goes during the same few days to catch a glimpse of the fields at their height before the grower cuts off the flowers. This he

opposite: Tulips were a costly commodity in the early 18th century, as seen by the handwritten notations on this list published by the Rotterdam merchant Henricus van der Heym in 1708. He was one of the most famous flower merchants of his time and had his own gardens on a plot of land outside the city. It was there that the 240 bulbs that he auctioned in 1708 had been produced. That sale brought in a total of 8662 florins (a few thousand dollars). The average price per bulb was 36 florins; some bulbs cost as much as 336 florins each. The bulletin reads: "Notice of Numbers, Names, and Weights of TULIPS, which will be sold on the 16th of May 1708, in the Garden of Henricus van der HEYM."

left: Those who visit Keukenhof enjoy its colorful floral exhibits in natural surroundings. Once a dense wood owned by Jacoba van Beirern, Keukenhof has been the showcase of the Dutch bulb industry since 1949. It is visited annually by hundreds of thousands of tourists from around the world.

right: This trilingual catalogue (French, German, and Dutch) was issued by the De Graaff brothers in Lisse in the late 18th century. For many years the largest bulb producer in The Netherlands, the firm closed in 1977.

above: During the 17th century, a hobby such as tulip growing could only be enjoyed by those wealthy enough to maintain stylish gardens. It was in gardens such as these, pictured here in a print entitled *A Dutch Garden* from the book *Hortus Floridus* by Chrispijn van de Passe (1594–1670), that the gardener could experiment with new plants and bulb varieties. Ownership of tulips granted prestige and status.

Three very different bouquets with one thing in common: the tasteful use of tulips. On the left, a pleasant, cheery bouquet for indoors; in the center, a bridal bouquet, festive yet modest; and on the facing page, a watercolor by Jan van Os (1744–1808) that captures the fleeting moment when the tulips are at the height of their glory.

must do as quickly as possible since they take strength from the bulb. He wants only to make sure that the flowers are of the right variety and that there are no mutations in the crop—he is interested in the bulb, not the blossom. The "heading" process is now done by machine, and very quickly all that remains of the colorful display are piles of blossoms along the edges of the fields (see page 23).

The creation of Keukenhof Park near Lisse improved this situation. For many years, a number of businessmen had toyed with the idea of creating a permanent, outdoor exhibition in the heart of the bulb region—a permanent showcase for the bulb profession. Their chance came in 1949, and they eagerly took it. Just to the west of the Lisse town line, near the train station, was a nature sanctuary owned by Count de Graaf van Lynden, originally part of the grounds of Keukenhof castle (see page 17). It was, for the most part, a dense wood.

Keukenhof Castle had been the scene of frequent balls and hunting parties. The bounty from hunting expeditions was prepared in the great kitchens for consumption at splendid banquets. The name Keukenhof means "Kitchen Yard"—the castle had become famous through its reputation for culinary excellence.

In 1949, Count van Lynden leased the Keuken Woods to the bulb growers, who wanted to transform it into a paradise of flowers. A simple gardener named Van der Lee resigned from his job at a nursery to take on the task of creating the gardens, which were to become his life's work. It was decided at the outset that any profits from operating

left: The tulip is a particularly effective motif when etched on crystal, as shown in this photograph of an antique water pitcher.

below and opposite: No vase is too elaborate for the tulip's stately charm, and these three pieces in blue Delft are no exception. The 3-foot-high, Chinese-inspired "tulip pagoda" on the extreme right dates from 1700 and is on permanent loan to the Rijksmuseum in Amsterdam.

Keukenhof would be reinvested in expansion and improvement of the park. Those who now manage the affairs of the park do so as volunteers, without any reward other than the satisfaction that comes from doing a good job.

The exhibitions at Keukenhof make it easy for the tourist to admire these glorious flowers at their very peak—and in peace. Special signs remind visitors that transistor radios are not permitted. Because of the tranquility of the park, the only sounds one hears are the murmurs of the visitors and the songs of birds.

The exhibit usually opens a week before Easter and closes six to eight weeks later. Should Easter be early, chances are everything will still have a light covering of snow. This is no reason to stay away, however, as the Keukenhof greenhouses are filled with blooming hyacinths, tulips, and daffodils.

Keukenhof is also the setting for outdoor exhibitions of sculpture by Dutch and foreign artists. Often, though, a conflict between flower lovers and art lovers arises. One exhibition included a fire-engine red metal construction, which was said to resemble a mailbox, and a row of white "things" with blinking lights that, tourists complained, looked like an open-air convenience station without walls. The constructions were quickly moved to a large open field away from the bulb exhibits, and the reputation of Beuken Lane, the main thoroughfare along which they had stood, was saved. Nevertheless, the sculpture exhibits attract a fair crowd each year, though not nearly so many as do the gloriously blooming bulbs.

Other Tulip Lands, Festivals, and Exhibits

There are a few other areas of The Netherlands that are noted for their bulbs. **Kennemerland,** located between the North Sea Canal and **Alkmaar** (north of Amsterdam), has very attractive bulb fields. The residents of the town of **Limmen** each year create floral mosaics and sculptures. The **Hortus Bulborum,** or bulb garden, in Limmen is a unique attraction; tulip varieties hundreds of years old still grow there. The Bulb Flower Museum, housed in a restored farmhouse, is a source of much fascinating information about the bulb industry and its history.

"Tulip strips" are to be found still farther north in the **Province of West Friesland.** These brilliant strips produce tulips that are well suited for greenhouses, particularly for florists who grow them solely as a source of cut flowers.

Tulips also grow in great quantities at the northernmost tip of The Netherlands around the towns of **Anna Paulowna** and **Breezand,** which are also known for their hyacinths. A floral sculpture competition is held here each year in late April. There is plenty of room in this part of the country, and so size, in addition to originality, is an important factor in the judges' decision.

But despite the attraction these activities in various parts of Holland hold, the **Corso,** or **Flower Festival,** put on each year in the bulb region near Haarlem, still draws the largest crowds. The Corso is a remarkable example of recycling: the festival is actually created out of

Three hundred years ago, the tulip was an international symbol used in many crafts and art forms. The design of the 17th-century Dutch tiles (*below*) was such that, when four of them were placed together, a star was formed at their center. The well-proportioned, 17th-century Chinese pitcher has a stylized tulip on the neck of the piece.

opposite: For those who must earn their living from tulips, the flower involves many demanding hours of hard work. Here they are "heading" the tulips, gathering up the petals, and carting them off to the side of the field.

the blossoms that have been cut off and would otherwise end up in piles alongside the fields.

The man who came up with the idea of doing something spectacular with these discarded flowers was not a bulb grower, nor did he come from the bulb region. Jos van Driel had been thinking for years of organizing a parade through the bulb region with floats made entirely of flowers. For more than 25 years now, Mr. van Driel has annually seen his dream come true. It was no easy task the first year, however. Floats had to be designed and armatures constructed. Van Driel himself designed each float, drew the plans, and personally supervised each detail of the undertaking. On the day of the parade, majorettes and marching bands from all over the region join in creating a festive occasion. The parade winds its way through the bulb-flowered landscape, starting at Haarlem, the City of Flowers, and finishing in Noordwijk, the popular coastal resort on the edge of the bulb region. Each year, more and more tourists come to record the Corso on film.

However, although the biggest display of bulbs comes in the spring, it is during the long winter months that one finds oneself especially longing for the gaiety of flowers. And so each year the **Hillegom Bulb Association** holds its **Kerstkeuring** ("Christmas Approval"), a display not actually organized for the general public. It is a gathering of professional growers who submit their boxes of tulips, daffodils, and hyacinths to a jury of experts whose job it is to judge the flowers' quality. The entries are placed on row after row of long tables, and, until the jury has finished its work, the public is not admitted.

The bulb flowers exhibited here must bloom earlier than they would had they been planted outdoors. In the case of some varieties, this can be as much as six months early. By carefully regulating the temperature in their greenhouses, growers can control the time at which the bulbs will flower—somewhat, at least. When the experts first enter the exhibition hall they can often tell at a glance whether it has been a good year. This Christmas show, an occasion for growers to get together to compare notes, attracts increasing numbers of flower lovers eager for a glimpse of spring. The exhibit often includes amaryllis, freesia, cyclamen, and irises.

The concept of a yearly "approval" goes back many years to the time when Sassenheim was the host town for the event known as Bloemlust (popularly known as Monte Carlo because of the gamble involved in growing tulips). After the building in which it was held burned down, the event was relocated in Hillegom.

The West Frisian Flora in Bovenkarspel has a greater following than does the Hillegom Show. It is held each year in February, and often visitors must fight winter snows for a chance to see the spring flowers. The Flora began modestly a half-century ago as a small, professional show and was held on one of the many "korfball" courts (a kind of golf game) common to the region. After the construction of an imposing auction hall complex in Bovenkarspel, the growers were able to move their exhibition indoors to the auction facilities, which were not in use during the winter months. Here again, the show began as a professional gathering, but was soon extended to include the general

The tulip's graceful shape has been captured in gold and silver countless times through the centuries. This 17th-century sconce is on display in the Utrecht Central Museum. Such costly pieces could be owned only by the wealthiest—those, for example, who could afford to live on such spendid estates as "Meerenburg" in the bulb region, pictured here in a contemporary print.

public. As a result, the West Frisian Flora has achieved international fame, and the number of its devotees increases each year. The halls are transformed into gardens, complete with paths, trees, shrubbery, fountains, and, of course, bulb flowers. Several villages hold local exhibits a week before the Flora as a preview of what can be expected there on a larger scale.

Nomenclature and Classification

But despite the attraction that these exhibits hold for the bulb tourist, Keukenhof remains the only exhibit where one can see a large assortment of bulb varieties assembled in one place. Even so, not *all* varieties are exhibited there, nor does it come even close to it. The *Classified List and International Register of Tulip Bulbs*, published in English by the Royal Dutch Bulb Society in Hillegom, lists some 2700 names, including a listing of 500 that are no longer available. The first and last entries of the *Classified List*, quoted here, indicate the precise information given each variety:

8 Aafje Heynis (F. Rijnveld & Sons Limited) exterior neyron-rose, edged primrose-yellow, inside primrose-yellow with neyron-rose to the base, base sulphur-yellow edged Blue, anthers purple. 1960.

6 Zwanenburg (Van Tubergen Ltd) pure white, base white, anthers black ($2n=24$) FCC Haarlem 1912.

Each entry in this 130-page social register of the tulip includes the variety, name, grower, and a detailed description of the color of the

Gold and silver are still popular media for re-creating the tulip—as an award, a trophy, or as this photograph shows, an official gift. Here, Her Royal Highness Princess Beatrix presents a silver tulip (enlarged to the *right*) to the Mayor of Cairo during her visit to Egypt in 1976. The Egyptian capital was also presented with enough bulbs to fill an entire park with Dutch flowers.

flower. The notation FCC stands for First Class Certificate. Some entries even include the number of chromosomes. In short, it contains all the information that the professional or amateur bulb grower will need.

The precision with which data about tulips are recorded is also reflected in the actual process of naming a new variety. Permission for the name must first be obtained from the Commission on Tulip Names if the tulip is to be sold commercially under that name. The Commission must give its approval to each new variety and its name before the bulb can be listed in the *Classified List*. Once so listed, the tulip's status has official recognition.

There are several ways in which names of varieties come about. Color is often the basis for a new name. The variety 'Deutschland' is black, red, and yellow—the colors of the German flag. 'Moonbeam,' 'Moonglow,' and 'Moonstruck' all have pale yellow in them, but 'Queen of the Night' and 'Black Beauty' are not as black as one might expect.

A tulip's name can often betray its age, as is the case with the handsome, oranged-tinted 'General De Wet,' named after one of the commanders of the Boer Wars in South Africa. According to the *Classified List*, this tulip was named in 1904. There are several other venerable varieties; 'Zomerschoon,' for example, was honored with the Royal Horticultural Society's Award of Merit in 1903.

Family names also are used. Dirk Lefeber, creator of the famous 'Madame Lefeber,' named this variety after both his wife and his

The tulip is found in and around the house, on sidewalks and along streets, and in the field. When the weather cooperates the tulip fields provide an unrivaled sight. The skyline of a city is paled by comparison with the bright splashes of color in the foreground.

mother. Dr. De Mol, who pioneered the use of radiation in the bulb industry, named a Parrot tulip after his wife, Estella Rijnveld. Another grower used a name that almost ended up in the family, but didn't quite make it: the maiden name of his high-school sweetheart who married another man.

International events also lead to the naming of a new variety. Such names as Neil Armstrong, President Kennedy, and Franklin D. Roosevelt have all found their way into the *Classified List*, as have older notables such as Shakespeare and Johann Strauss.

Men have for centuries tried to classify the tulip's many sizes and shapes. Rembertus Dodonaeus (1517–85) lists tulips as early, mid-season, and late-blooming tulips in his *Cruydeboeck* ("Plant Book," 1554), a division that is still used in the *Classified List*.

New varieties of tulips can come about in one of two ways. They can occur as a chance mutation or "sport" as is often the case with the Parrot tulips. Such a tulip, which differs radically from the parent tulip, begins its own life as a new variety. More generally, however, a new variety is created through the efforts of a bulb grower or horticulturist (see pages 72, 73). This process begins with the tulip seeds (called "ovules"), which are located in the ovary of the tulip under the stigma. The breeder takes pollen from the anther of one variety and carefully implants it in the ovary of another, using tweezers or a very small paint brush. As soon as the fertilized seeds begin to swell, they are removed and planted with the utmost care and precision in small containers.

26

Once modern procedures were established, the number of new tulip varieties got out of hand, and in 1929 the first publication of the *Classified List* attempted to organize the situation. (Work had actually been completed on the *List* long before 1929, but publication had been delayed by World War I.)

Today the tulip family is divided into classes, each of which includes many varieties. Thus, one often sees such labels as "SET Yellow Prince" (Single Early Tulip *class*, 'Yellow Prince' *variety*) and 'TT Manchester' (Triumph Tulip, 'Manchester').

The **Single Early Tulips** include some of the oldest varieties (see page 82). The 'Yellow Prince' is none other than the 'Gele Prins,' which dates from 1785. Many more of these varieties, which are still available commercially, come to us from the latter half of the 19th century. The Christmas tulip 'Brilliant Star' is an example of this group.

The **Double Early Tulips** also have a long, but often obscure, history (see pages 84, 85). One of the most famous of this group was the 'Murillo,' developed in 1850 and now the "grandmother" of many new varieties in which there is no trace of the original pink color.

The **Mendel Tulips** were named after the world-famous, yet humble, monk Gregor Johann Mendel (1822–84) whose experiments with pea plants laid the foundations of modern genetic theory (see page 87).

Darwin Tulips were named after Charles Darwin, founder of the theory of evolution (see pages 91–95). These tulips, which entered the

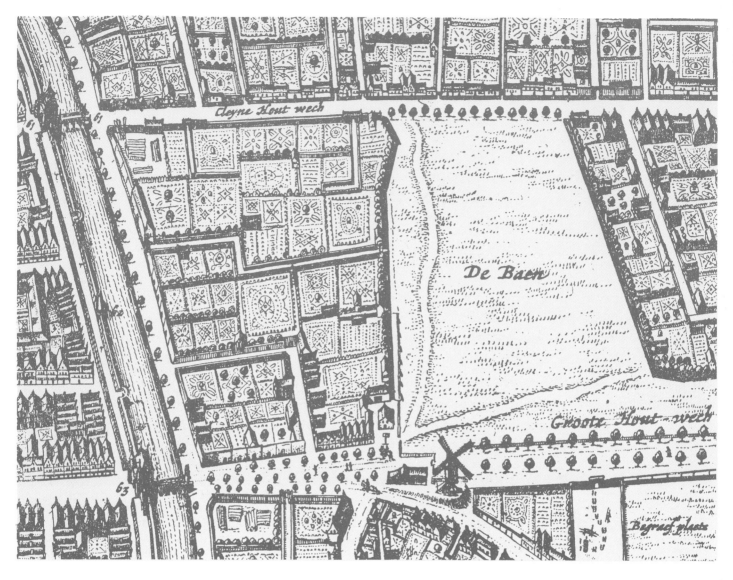

In the first half of the 17th century, quite a few tulip gardens were maintained just outside the walls of Haarlem, as this map shows. The streets of Haarlem recall the names of early pioneers in the bulb profession: Krelage, Voorhelm, and Schneevoogt.

market in their original state (not cross-pollinated)—a character that they share with tulips imported from Turkey—were first introduced to the European market by a Belgian named Lille who had a flourishing business in the village of Rijssel. He later sold his interest in the firm to the Dutchman Krelage in Haarlem. Krelage was convinced that what we now know as Darwins would become a completely new class of tulips, a claim disputed at the time by English horticulturists. It seems that the first Darwins imported by Krelage were not strong and wilted quickly. The Darwin became popular only much later, after it had established a reputation as a handsomely shaped, exotically colored tulip. Its long, firm stem made it ideal as a cutting flower.

Triumph Tulips, the result of various crossings, appeared on the market at about the same time as the Mendel tulips (see pages 88, 89). They were so successful, both as a cutting flower and as a garden flower, that they quickly earned the right to their name.

The **Species Tulips,** like the Darwins, are "primitive" tulips that originate in the Middle East and Central Asia (see pages 102–107, 109). When they first arrived in Holland from Turkey in the 16th century, it was obvious that they had been carefully cultivated. The origin of these flowers, however, could only be guessed (see Chapter 2).

Dutch growers who were seriously involved in increasing the assortment of tulips were convinced that a search for tulips in their natural habitats would provide the new material needed for their work. The Haarlem grower Van Tubergen, who was by profession a tobacco merchant but was destined for fame as a bulb grower, sent expeditions

These two fine antiques, an octagonal table top and a side chair, show the influence of the tulip on furniture design.

to the far, uncharted corners of the earth where the wild tulip was to be found. These expeditions went as far east as China and Tibet, and into regions where they were exposed to harsh living conditions and even danger. Between the 1880s and the start of World War I in 1914, men such as Sintenis, Haberhauer, Manissadjian, and Graeber, who for 25 years made Tashkent his home base, sent a continuous stream of new varieties back to Holland. Just before the outbreak of the war, Joseph Haberhauer shipped a unique collection of Asian bulbs back to Europe. The shipment was held up at a border and never reached its destination—years of work lost forever.

The *tulipa* from Central Asia and Asia Minor that did arrive in Europe provided new varieties for breeding. The Fosteriana (see page 104), Kaufmanniana (see page 105), and Greigii (see pages 102, 103) tulips were the progenitors of completely new types of tulips that have become famous for their rare colors, uniquely shaped petals, and exotic leaves. The new kinds were eagerly greeted by the public, who sought them for their short stems and early bloom. They were ideal for borders and rock gardens.

The **Species Tulips** have such enchanting names as 'Billietians' (from Switzerland), 'Borszczowi' (Central Asia), 'Dammaniana' (Lebanon), and 'Leichtlini' (Kashmir) (see pages 102–107). They are all attractive; the 'Leichtlini,' for example, is coral-red on the outside and a creamy-yellow on the inside and measures 20 inches high. The 'Nitida' from Buchara grows no higher then 2 inches. The 'Primulina' (Eastern Algeria), with its fragrant flowers, is no longer cultivated, but

right: The tulipomania of the 17th century was satirized on canvas as well as on the printed page. This painting, *Flora's Wagon of Idiots* by Hendrik Gerritszoon Pot (1585–1657), is now in the collection of the Frans Hals Museum in Haarlem. It was obviously copied from an earlier engraving (see page 32) that has been attributed to Chrispijn van de Passe.

above: This public notice appeared in January 1637 just before the end of the tulip craze: "Warning to all good citizens of our beloved country against the threat of those who call themselves Florists. . . ."

its beauty is preserved in other tulips developed from it—for example, 'Acuminata' with spiral-shaped leaves. It is common for these types to have more than one flower on each stem. The 'Biflora' from the Caucasus, for example, has five off-white flowers on each stem; the dwarf tulip 'Pulchella' (from Taurus) and the 'Saxatils' (from Crete) often have three or more flowers per stem. The remarkable 'Praecox' has a bright red, cone-shaped flower.

The **Lily-Flowered Tulip**, with petals that gracefully arch out away from the stem, is centuries old (see pages 96, 97). The 'Retroflexa' was first introduced by Vincent van der Vinne (1799–1879) of Haarlem, a well-known painter and flower expert. Many crossings with Darwins were carried out during the first decade of this century. Although they were once classed as Cottage tulips, the Lily-flowered tulips now have their own class because of the large number of their varieties.

Cottage Tulips (or **Single Late Tulips**) owe their name to the story that they originated in English cottage gardens, although this is not known for sure (see pages 98, 99). They include some exotic varieties that are often called "orchid tulips." These are distinguished from regular Cottages by fringed petals and, sometimes, three to five flowers on one stem.

The **Rembrandt Tulips** have the same appearance as the broken (or mutant) tulips of earlier eras that were the result of viral infections in the bulb (see pages 56, 57). Strictly speaking, the name Rembrandt applies only to Darwins that have been broken as a result of viruses; however, the *Classified List* registers all broken tulips as Rembrandts.

opposite: This engraving, ascribed to Chrispijn van de Passe (1594–1670), is a satire on almost every aspect of the "wind trade." It includes a sailing wagon, an invention of the famous physicist Simon Stevin, which has an obvious connection with the wind trade. Seated in the wagon is the flower goddess Flora with three tulips in her right hand: the 'Semper Augustus,' the 'General Bol,' and the 'Admiral van Hoorn.' The three men in the wagon are each wearing Flora's Dunce Cap. They are in the company of two ladies, Vergaeral ("Collect All") and Ydel Hope ("Vain Hope"). Ydel Hope holds a broken string that had been attached to a bird now flown away. To avoid every possibility of a misunderstanding, the bird is labeled "vain hope has flown away."

The wagon is decorated with the emblems of the inns in various cities where the florists' meetings were held. The mast is topped by a banner that shows a fool's cap and three tulips. A monkey climbs the mast and clearly lets his opinion of the whole scene be known.

Men and women who, as a caption tells us, "want to sail along, too," follow the wagon from behind. At their feet lie a weaver's tools, silent testimony to the many, many weavers who gave up their profession to enter the wind trade. Tulips (each individually named) lie strewn around the sailing-wagon.

Each corner of the print contains smaller prints showing localities where the meetings were held: top left, the Pottebackershof, probably in Gouda; top right, the Hoorn Comparitie; and bottom left, that at Haarlem. The print in the lower right hand corner shows a sales transaction. The caption reads: "Even though a crazy deed's been done, we'll seek good advice, and not for fun." And then, puckishly, "Did someone really mean that?"

The print of the Hoorn group (*below left*) shows a man driving a carriage away from the meeting, probably to a hiding place near Vianen to escape his creditors.

An interesting detail of the Haarlem print is of the women in the background making waffles (*below right*). This is meant to symbolize the wealth of the gentlemen around the table who can afford to eat expensive food, paid for with the premium prices received from every transaction.

Compariti der Bloemiſten tot Horn

Comparity der Bloemiſten tot Harlem

Parrot Tulips date back at least to the late 17th century (see pages 100, 101): the 'Amiral de Constantinople' of 1772 actually developed from the 'Admiral van Constantinople' of 1672, for example. Although the precise origin of the Parrot tulips, also known as Parakeet tulips, is unknown, it is believed that they have developed from Cottage tulips. Originally, the Parrots were not popular because their heavy flowers caused the stems to bend, and they also had bizarre color combinations. The first popular Parrot was a sport (chance mutation)— the sensational salmon-colored 'Fantasy.' Since that time Parrot tulips have improved in both color and form, without losing any of the picturesque charm of their "Featheriness."

Actually, each Parrot variety is a sport developed from Single Early, Triumph, and Darwin tulips. An exception is the 'Estella Rijnveld,' developed by Dr. De Mol through radiation treatments; but it, too, is a mutation of another mutation, the Parrot 'Red Champion,' which itself was a Darwin sport.

Another venerable tulip classification is the **Double Late** or **Peony-Flowered Tulip,** which was at one time too heavy for its stem. Improvements were achieved, and it is now a type well suited for the garden.

What motivates growers to seek improved and perfected tulips? New markets must be developed, of course, and the older, less popular varieties should be replaced. But money is not the only object—it all comes down to love and dedication and a devotion to the flower known as the tulip.

right: Committees of tulip experts existed even in 18th-century Turkey, as this contemporary Turkish miniature illustrates. They set the standards by which the quality of the flower was to be judged.

below: This 17th-century Turkish book listed the characteristics of the "ideal" tulip. Turkish flower-lovers preferred tulips with an almond-shaped blossom and pointed petals.

2 The Tulip in History

right: Sultan Suleiman I (1494–1566) was a poet, philosopher, and lover of flowers. During his reign, the tulip was the flower of the Turkish court. The 1652 book *The Royal Envoy to the Great Suleiman* gave a different picture of him, however: "This is the cruel despot who drinks the blood of his sons as though it were nectar," reads a caption under this engraving.

left: The tulip was a common theme in 17th-century Turkish folklore, as shown by this example of folk art in the Austrian National Library in Vienna. The stylized garden is done in cut paper and paints.

For centuries, men have attempted to trace the history of the tulip, a history which is often obscured by the lack of reliable documentation. We do know that the tulip originated thousands of years ago in an area that stretches from the coasts of the Mediterranean well past the borders of China (see page 109). The map is blank, however, when it comes to sketching in the journey of the tulip from a wild flower in China to a cultivated one in Constantinople.

We know little about the flower before its emergence in the Middle East, and we have scant idea of what it looked like before cultivation by the Turks. The first tulips that came from Turkey in the 16th century were not wild flowers. They were highly cultivated products that, without a doubt, were the result of experimentation, expertise, and experience—ready for the consumer.

While knowledge of the tulip before the 16th century is vague, occasionally it appears in illustration to give us a glimpse of its past. An illuminated Bible dating from the 12th century has been found in which the tulip figures among a variety of flower motifs used to decorate the letters. And during World War II a mural (probably dating from the 15th century) of the Madonna and Child surrounded by tulips was found among the rubble of bombed Coventry Cathedral.

The Age of Tulips in Turkey

The history of the tulip as we know it, however, begins during the 16th century in Turkey, the time of the Ottoman Empire and of Sultan

right: The Flemish nobleman Ogier Ghiselin de Busbecq (1522–92), envoy to the court of Sultan Suleiman I, introduced the tulip to Western Europe. His friend Carolus Clusius grew tulips in Prague and in Leiden.

left: De Busbecq records in the diary reproduced here that he saw tulips blooming in Turkey in midwinter. He did not describe the Turkish population in very flattering terms.

AUGER GISLEEN BUSBEEQ. 49

ken zeggen aldaar met handen gemaakt te wezen, ter gedagtenis van de veldflagen, die aldaar veel geflagen zijn, en dat 'er de verflagene menfchen begraven leggen. In dees togt volgden wy meeft den oever van den Heber, die ons aan de regter-hand by bleef, en lieten den Heem, die in de zee uitloopt, aan de flinkker-hand leggen. Eindelijk fcheepten wy over den Heber, en quamen over de beroemde brug van Muftapha te Hadrianopolen, by de Turkken Endrene genoemd. Eer de Kaizar dees ftad vergroote, en na fijnen naam liet noemen, was fy Orefta gezeid. S'is gelegen by de t'zamenvloejing van Mariz, of den Heber, en de rivierkens Tunfa en Harda, die daar na in d' Ægæifche zee uitloopen. Voor zoo veel fy in haar oude wallen leid, is ze de grootfte niet; maar de voorfteden, en huizen, die 'er de Turkken aan gebouwd hebben, maken ze tot een groot lighaam. Een dag te Hadrianopolen verbleven hebbende, gaven wy ons op weg na Konftantinopolen, 't geen ons nu begon te naderen, en de laatfte handeling van onze reis mogt gezeid werden. Door dees plaatzen reizende, zagen wy overal een grooten hoop bloemen, als narçiffen, hyaçinthen, en die de Turkken Tulipan noemen, daar wy ons zeer over verwonderden, nadien 't in 't midden

C   van

50   Den Kaizarlijkken Gezant,

van de winter was. Griekkenland is zeer overvloedig in narçiffen en hyaçinthen, die zoo fterk van reuk zijn, dat f'iemand, die 't ongewoon is, laftig vallen. De tulpaans hebben geen, of zeer weinig reuk, en werden alleen na haar fchoonheid, of verfcheide koleuren, gefchat. De Turkken houden zeer veel van bloemen, en durven voor een fraje wel eenige afperen geven. Sy koften my ook wel wat, als fy my gefchonkken wierden: want ik moft dan altijd eenige afperen tot dankbaarheid fchenkken. Die met de Turkken om wil gaan, moet ook geen ander rekening maken, als dat hy, in haar palen komende, terftond fijn beurs moet openen, en niet eer fluiten, voor dat hy ze wederom verlaten heeft. Als dit geld-zajen nog niet vrugteloos is, heeft men zig geenzins te beklagen. Maar dit 's een zekere vrugt, die fy voortbrengd, dat ze der Turkken wreeden, en ontmenfchten aard, alleen vermurwen kan. Met dezen zang werden de Turkken in flaap gezuft, die anders geen menfchen zouden mogen genaken. Zonder dit was Turkkyen zoo onmogelijk te bewonen, als de plaatzen, die om haar onlijdelijkke hit, of koude, onbewoond blijven. Te middeweg, tuffchen Konftantinopolen en Hadrianopolen, leid een ftedeken Chiurli genoemd, en befaamd

Suleiman I (1494–1566; see page 35). It was during this period that the bulb was tamed, cultivated for its shape and color, to give pleasure to the Sultan and his entourage.

During Suleiman's reign, Constantinople, once the glittering capital of the powerful Eastern Roman Empire, became the seat of the Sublime Porte; and the cross of Christianity was replaced by the crescent of Islam. Suleiman's empire included a large area of the Balkans and the countries around the Black Sea. It stretched out as far as the Persian Gulf and included the southern shores of the Mediterranean Sea and all of Asia Minor.

At that time Constantinople had the reputation of being the most beautiful city of the world. Built on a series of hills, its position between two major bodies of water contributed to its having a power and a prestige that even Rome never achieved. It became the crossroads of trade, culture, and political power.

The Turkish Sultans built their *seraglios* ("harems") on a peninsula that jutted into the Sea of Marmaris. This city within a city, a complex of buildings surrounded by magnificient gardens, housed a large staff of servants, slaves, and the eunuchs who looked after the needs of some 300 veiled odalisques. Suleiman was an exceptionally gifted ruler and a man of many contrasts: a skillful military strategist, a poet of merit, a statesman who admired Aristotle, and a lover faithful to the slave Roxelana, who was officially second in the harem hierarchy. He appreciated everything that grew and bloomed, especially the tulip— the official flower of his court. He maintained extensive gardens (see

page 35) at his summer residence in Adrianople (now Edirne) along the banks of the Maritsa River.

Suleiman was followed by a succession of sultans, each the son of a slave; and gradually, conditions within the empire deteriorated. Against the background of unimaginable wealth distributed among relatively few, the tulip reigned as though it were the symbol of the empire. Money and manpower were unlimited for the sultan and his entourage, who enjoyed their horticultural hobby without restraint. When Sultan Moerad III died in 1595, his son hurried by boat to the funeral of his father, but not without first arranging for the planting of a half-million hyacinths at the spot where his barge would dock.

The era of the tulip reached its apex during the reign of Ahmed III (1703–30; see page 38). Ahmed's Grand Vizier Mehmed was known both as Lâlizari, "lover of tulips," and a Sehukjufê Perweran, "lover of flowers." It is known that Ahmed actually imported tulip bulbs from Holland, thereby bringing the bulb full circle.

Regardless of what the Dutch growers were able to accomplish in those days, the Turks were still the undisputed experts in the art of tulip growing. Strict laws regulated the cultivation and sale of the flower. During the reign of Sultan Ahmed III, it was forbidden to buy or sell tulips outside of the capital. Those who broke this law were punished by exile, a mild punishment compared with the various means of torture that could have been applied. The Frenchman Fachat, a tulip merchant in Constantinople, once remarked that in Turkey a tulip bulb was more highly valued than a human life.

The tulip era in Turkey reached its apex during the reign of Sultan Ahmed III (1703–30). Tulips were even reimported from Holland. This painting by J. B. Vanmour, in Amsterdam's Rijksmuseum, depicts the arrival of the Dutch Ambassador Cornelis Calkoen (1695–1764) at the Court of the Sultan.

In his book *Traité des tulipes* (1760), J. P. d'Ardène tells of a letter written in 1726 by Monsieur d'Andresol, the French envoy to the Turkish court, describing the unique position the tulip held at court. D'Andresol estimated that there were at least a half-million flower bulbs in the Grand Vizier's gardens.

Each year, the Seraglio was the scene of a glittering tulip festival, held during full moon. Hundreds of exquisite vases were filled with the most expensive tulips available and were placed on stands decorated with crystal balls filled with colored water. Crystal lanterns cast an enchanting glow throughout the gardens. Canaries and nightingales in cages hung on branches to delight the guests with their song—a song that was drowned out now and then by music from the Janissary, the Sultan's guard. Guests were required to wear colors that harmonized with the flowers. One evening of the festival was reserved for the ladies of the harem, who organized a charity bazaar with their lord and master as the only customer. A tulip festival is still held annually in Istanbul, the old city on the "Golden Horn." It is a reminder of a bygone, glorious era, but oddly enough, there are no tulips to be found anywhere at the festival.

This period of Turkish history has become known as the Age of Tulips. While such festivities advanced the status of the flower, they were also a drain on the national economy. Jealous adversaries conspired against Ahmed and brought his wordly existence to an end.

Tulip worship did not stop here, however. History records that Sultan Abdul-Hamid I gave a splendid tulip party on the occasion of

An extravagent tulip festival was held in
1783 to mark the birth of Abdul-Hamid I's
son, who later reigned as Mahmud II. It is
said that the mother of the child was none
other than the French Lady Aimée Dubucq
de Rivéry, a cousin of Joséphine de
Beauharnais, wife of Napoleon. *left:*
Aimée. *center:* Mahmud II. *right:* Prince
Selim, cousin and successor of Abdul-
Hamid, who was said to have had an affair
with Aimée after the death of Abdul-
Hamid.

the birth of the son who would later reign as Mahmud II. The mother
of the child is said to have been none other than the French-born
Aimée Dubucq de Rivéry (see above), a cousin of Joséphine de
Beauharnais, wife of Napoleon. Brought up on the island of
Martinique where she had attended convent school, she was on a
return voyage to France when her ship was hijacked by a group of
Algerian pirates. The Bey of Algiers was so taken with Aimée's beauty
that he took personal responsibility for her and, wishing to remain on
good terms with the sultan, offered the lovely Frenchwoman to the
Turkish ruler for his harem. It is rumored that the French concubine
became the power behind the 60-year-old Abdul-Hamid's throne and,
through her correspondence with Joséphine, influenced French-
Turkish relations. Still, as a woman of the harem, she could only
observe her son's birthday party from behind a screen.

The Turks carefully recorded all existing tulip varieties, a total
of 1588, and new ones as they came along, in *Ferahengiz*, the oldest
tulip book known. The Grand Vizier Mehmed Lâlizari later
published a volume called *Mizanul Ezhar*, which included 1323 names
names of tulips and described many varieties that originated in Aleppo,
Shiraz, and Turkmenistan. Mehmed's book shows that the Turks were
as creative in the naming of tulips as the Dutch would be hundreds of
years later.

Tulips had to meet certain standards if they were to have a chance
of finding their way into a royal garden or a Grand Vizier's tulip book
(see page 34):

Carolus Clusius (1526–1609), curator of the botanical gardens in Leiden, was the most important horticulturist to work with tulips at that time. To the right is a reproduction of a lithographic illustration from the book *Album van Eeden*, now in the Library of the Royal Dutch Bulb Society.

1. The flower had to resemble an almond.
2. Each petal had to resemble a dagger.
3. The petals had to be smooth and firm.
4. Each flower had to have six petals, all of identical size.
5. The petals had to touch each other.
6. The three innermost petals had to be narrower than the three outermost.
7. The anthers and ovaries had to be hidden from sight.
8. The flower had to stand erect.

Just as today there are Committees of experts and professionals to judge the quality of various decorative plants so also were there inspectors in the Ottoman empire who established standards for color and color patterns (breaks), for size and form.

Tulips Come to Europe

During the second half of the 16th century, when Turkey was still the land of the tulip, the Belgian diplomat Ogier Ghiselin de Busbecq (1522–92, see page 36), envoy of the German emperor, wrote enthusiastically to his friends in Europe of the beauty of the tulips that he saw in Constantinople. His friend Carolus Clusius (see above), then prefect of the Royal Medicinal Garden in Prague, showed great interest in the bulbs. And so de Busbecq sent his friend some tulip seeds, and that was the event that marked the introduction of the tulip to Europe. Clusius eventually resigned his post in Prague and

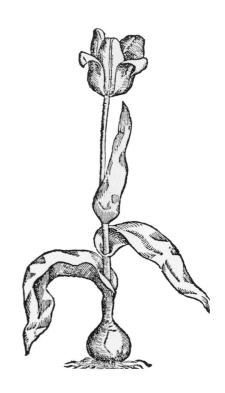

left: A tulip illustration by Conrad Gesner (1516–65) from a book published by his friend Valerius Cordus in 1561. The Swiss Gesner was a many-sided horticulturist who was far ahead of his time. He tried to classify plants according to the shape of their flowers.

center: This is the colophon of the famous Antwerp printer Plantijn. Plantijn possessed a large number of woodcuts which he used for the illustration of books by the famous horticulturists Dodonaeus, Lobelius, and Clusius; and one often finds the same print in books by different authors.

right: This illustration of a tulip is by the Flemish horticulturist Rembert Dodonaeus (1517–85). His books are important sources for tracing the history of decorative plants and flowers. The first of them was published in Mechelen in 1554.

emigrated to The Netherlands. He was offered the position of curator of the botanical gardens, or "Hortus," in Leiden. When Clusius arrived, however, these gardens were still in their infancy and achieved their fame mainly through his work. The Hortus is still carefully maintained and is open to the public.

In those days, a garden such as the Hortus was the primary source of herbs and plants used as medicine in the treatment of disease. Because the men in charge of such gardens were scientists by profession, they were interested in experiments with plants. But Clusius planted tulips for the sheer pleasure of watching these exotic plants grow. He and de Busbecq never knew that these strange and amusing bulbs would one day spread throughout the world.

Some say that Clusius sold bulbs at scandalously high prices, others that he refused to sell them at all. From what we know about him, the latter possibility seems more likely. There were other men, though, who saw the bulb's commercial potential, but hard as they tried, they could not convince the stubborn curator, Clusius, to make tulip bulbs available to them. Determined to gain possession of at least a few of them, they sneaked into the botanical gardens one day and stole a number of bulbs. Clusius, disgusted with the whole affair, gave up his work with tulips, never to grow them again.

While it was in 1575 that Clusius made public his knowledge of the tulip's existence, it had actually first been noted in Europe fifteen years earlier by the German, Conrad Gesner (see above), who had seen it in a friend's garden in Augsburg. Clusius's friend Rembert

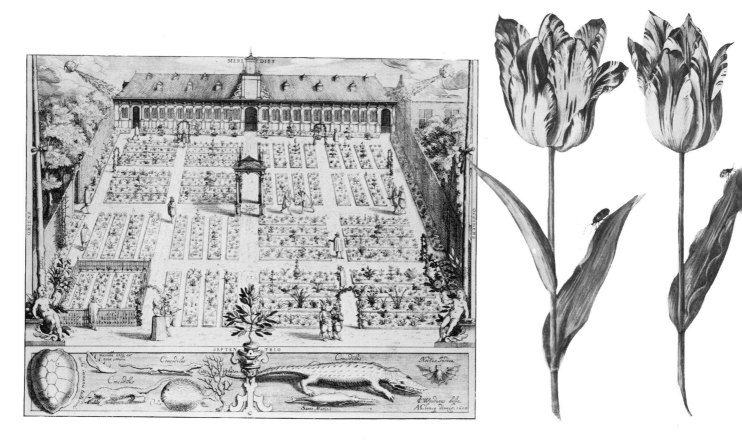

Dodoen, better known as Dodonaeus (see page 41), had also described the tulip as early as 1567.

In 1582, the Englishman Richard Hakluyt wrote of various flowers named "tulipas" that were then being imported from Austria. The famous English horticulturist John Parkinson (see page 45) included four engravings of tulips in his *Paradisi in Sole,* complete with an extensive description of the flower he called "the turkes cap" (i.e. turban) or *lale,* Turkish for "tulip."

At about the same time, the *Apparatus Plantorius* (1632) by P. Lauremberg, published in Frankfurt, included a number of especially handsome illustrations of the tulip. It is said that Lauremberg's daughter, an artist, was so taken with the tulip's beauty, that she once stole into the garden of her father's neighbor, Count von Ruitner, to pick some of the tulips growing there. The girl was none other than Maria Sibylla Merian who lived in Holland for many years and became well known there as a painter of floral masterpieces. While in Holland, she lived as a member of the pious religious sect, the Labadists. She traveled to the wilds of Surinam and other areas of South America to observe flora and fauna there. Characteristic is her use of butterflies and seashells as accents in her paintings of flowers (see pages 43, 75).

Tulips in The Netherlands

At first, the tulip was prized only as a natural curiosity, as a focus of scientific inquiry. In later years, however, tulips became a hobby for

the extremely rich, who were able to maintain large gardens where they could experiment with exotic plants.

The establishment of the East India Company in 1602 marked the dawn of an era of prosperity for The Netherlands, for those, at least, who were in power—the merchants and the regents. The stately residences of wealthy patricians rose along the canals of Amsterdam; country houses were built along the River Vecht and in the Kennemerland region; and the wealthy became wealthier. Everything they touched turned to gold.

Other professions flourished as a result of this new-found wealth. Along with the great success of the shipping industry came the need for middlemen, small businessmen who could cater to the needs of the rich—lawyers, notaries, doctors, pharmacists, and jewelers. Scholars, artists, and poets also thrived on the patronage of the wealthy: Rembrandt, Frans Hals, Jan Steen, Jacob van Ruysdael, Meyndert Hobbema, the writers Vondel and Hooft, and the philosopher Spinoza.

There were those in the society, though, who did not share this prosperity: ordinary folk, such as stevedores, laborers, servants; and those on the fringes of 17th-century Dutch society—the unemployed, vagabonds, beggars. Many of them lived in hovels without decent food or clothing, but with luxuries in view and just out of reach.

Life for the privileged classes was not as carefree as it might seem. Money could buy houses, servants, art and clothing, but there was one thing it could not buy—health. For all the sophistication of the Golden Age, effective medicine and public hygiene were all but nonexistent.

left: Title page of the 1637 book *Samen-spraeck tusschen Waermondt ende Gaergoedt* ("Discussion between Warmond and Gaargoed"). This little book gives an often-amusing view of the wind trade. It was reprinted in 1643 and again in 1734, when there was a threat of a "wind trade" involving hyacinths.

below: This 17th-century map shows the bulb region before it was known as such. A portion of it shows the area around the villages of Lisse and Noordwijkerhout. The Heereweg appears between Meerenburg and Castle Teylingen, once the home of Jacoba van Beirern.

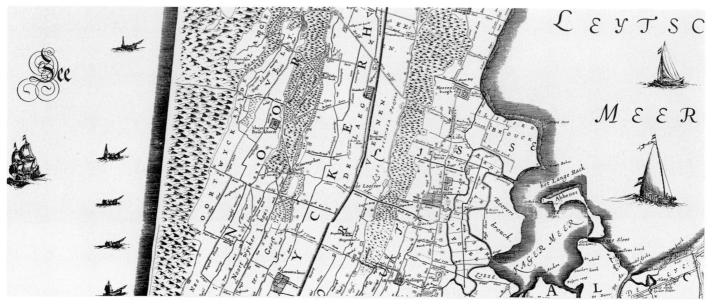

Infectious diseases struck without warning and decimated the population of a town or city within days. There was no herb strong enough to combat plague and smallpox.

Also, little could be done to remove the constant threat of invasion by foreign troops. The occupation of Holland first by the Spanish and then by the French was proof of that.

Yet it was under such conditions that a certain reckless *joie de vivre* developed and permeated the fragile society of 17th-century Holland. "Pick the rose before it dies," was a common saying —although the "in" flower was the tulip rather than the rose.

The rarity of the tulip restricted its ownership to such personages as Adriaen Pauw, Knight, Lord of Heemstede, Bennebroek, and Niewerkerk, Director of the East Indies Company, Presiding Counsel and Treasurer of the Domain of Holland and West Friesland, Keeper of the Great Seal of Holland, and envoy of the States General to foreign courts. His modest residence just outside Haarlem was surrounded by immense gardens that, according to the local historian Nicolaas van Wassenaar, "contained a profusion of tulips clustered around a mirrored gazebo." The mirrors gave the illusion of multiplying flowers. This trick was used in many 17th-century Dutch gardens. Van Wassenaar also records that "among the many costly flowers to be found in the garden is the 'Semper Augustus.' This year it is the most expensive flower on the market. It has sold for thousands of florins, and at those prices, people say they have been cheated." What

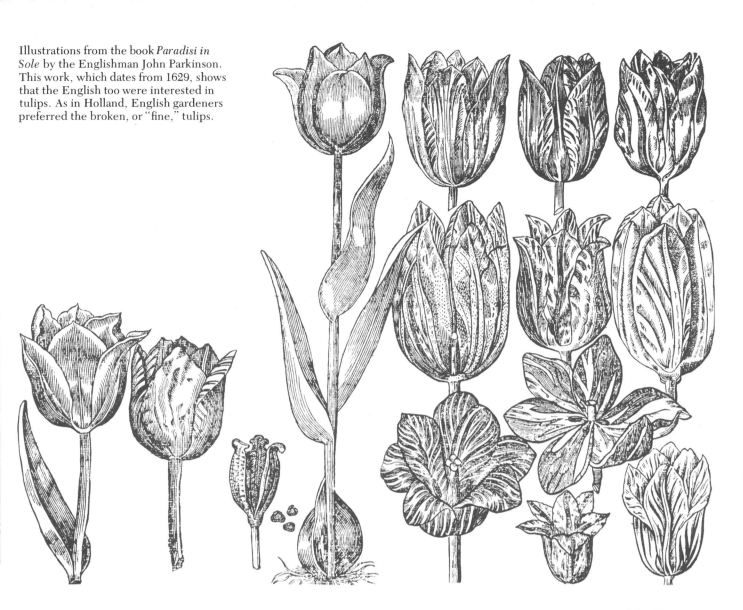

Dr. Pauw did not know when he sold his 'Semper Augustus' bulb (see page 43) was that it had reproduced itself two-fold, and he could have doubled his money.

Prices for the 'Semper Augustus' were astronomical. In 1641, an owner of 10 bulbs was offered 12,000 florins, but he declined to sell them. Consequently, in 1642 there were only one dozen bulbs on the market, with a value of 1,200 florins apiece.

Tulips in the 17th Century

The assortment of bulbs available in the 17th century was limited by today's standards. Attempts were made to classify the existing varieties, but the books that resulted have little in common with the modern *Classified List and International Register of Tulip Names*.

During the 17th century, the names of tulips were often chosen to indicate the quality of the flower. The Bailiff of Kennemerland, for example, acquired an exceptionally attractive tulip, which he christened the 'Admiral.' Tulips of approximately the same quality subsequently came to be known by similar names, and sometimes included the name of the locality in which the bulb had been produced; for example, the 'Admiral da Costa,' 'Admiral van Enkhuysen,' 'Admiral Liefkins,' and 'Admiral van der Eyk,' all tulips that date from this period. Others named their tulips after Generals; there was a 'General Nieuwlander,' 'General de Man,' and even a 'General of Generals.' Some remarkable and often amusing names turn

Tooneel ban FLORA.

Vertonende :

Grondelijcke Redens-onderfoekinge,

vanden

HANDEL DER FLORISTEN.

Ghefpeelo/ op de fpjeucke ban Anthonius de Guevara :
Een voorfichtich eerlijck man ; fal altijt meer ghedulden,
dan ftraffen.

T'famen gefteld; mits/datter dagelijr :

Uyt haat : fpruyt fmaad.

Noch is hier by-gevoegt de Lijfte van eenige *Tulpaen* vercocht aende meeft-
biedende tot Alcmaer op den 15 Februarij 1637.   Item 't Lof-dicht
van *Calliope*, over de Goddinne FLORA, &c.

t'AMSTERDAM,
Ghedzuckt by Iooft Broerfz. Boeck-dzucker inde Gzaebe-ftraet/
inde Dzuckerpe/ Anno 1637.

COPYE
Van een Notoriael accoort, gemaeckt tuffchen
de Gecommitteerde der

FLORISTEN
Van verfcheyde Steden.

up on lists of 17th-century tulips: 'Rattebeet' ('Rat Bite') and 'Serij Naeby' (Turkish for "almost silk") are but two examples.

The 17th-century tulips looked very little like today's flowers, and what slight resemblance there is is limited to the Rembrandt (or broken) tulips. Some of these centuries-old varieties are still to be seen at the Hortus Bulborum in Limmen, Holland, where the antique splendor of these tulips is carefully preserved.

At the height of the tulip's popularity, in the 16th and 17th centuries, the most sought-after bulbs were the so-called broken or "fine" tulips with striped, spotted, or flame-patterned petals (see pages 56, 57).

A tulip developed from a seed was usually monochrome at first. Later, as it came in contact with viral infections, the desired breaks gradually developed. To the 17th century tulip lover, monochrome tulips just did not count.

The exceptionally beautiful illustrations of the multicolored tulips dating from that period (see pages 2, 43, 56, 57) are silent testimony to the spell these flowers held over their admirers. Fortunately, many early tulip books and illustrations have come down to us and provide a unique view of those early times. One fine example is the tulip book by Judith Leyster, the Haarlem artist who was both a niece and a pupil of Frans Hals. The book is now on display in the Judith Leyster Museum in Haarlem.

Given the degree to which such tulips were valued, it is not surprising that standards were established in an effort to classify tulips by quality. This proved to be almost an impossible task because the

Lijste van eenighe Tulpaen/

Verkocht aende meest-biedende/ op den 5. Februarij 1637. Op de Sael vande Nieuwe Schutters Doelen/ int bywesen vande E. Heeren Wees-Meesteren/ ende Voochden/ ghecoomen van Wouter Bartelmesz. Winckel/ in sijn Leven Castelent vande Oude Schutters Doelen tot Alckmaer.

Inden eersten.

Een veranderde Botter-man van 563. Asen gheplant.	263.
De Schipio, van 82. Asen geplant.	400.
Een Parragon van Delft of Mols-wijck, van 354. Asen gheplant.	605.
Een Bruyne Purper, van 320. Asen gheplant.	2025.
Een Viseroy, van 410. Asen geplant.	3000.
De Monastier, van 510. Asen geplant.	830.
Een vroeghe Blijenburgher, van 443. Asen gheplant.	1300.
Een Gouda, van 187. Asen gheplant.	1330.
Een Iulius Ceser, van 82. Asen geplant.	650.
De Tulpa Kos, van 477. Asen geplant.	300.
Een Botterman, van 400. Asen geplant.	405.
Een Schapesteyn, van 246. Asen geplant.	375.
Een Bellaart, van 399. Asen gheplant.	1520.
Een Parragon van Delft of Mols-wijck, van 294. Asen gheplant.	650.
Een Ameraal Liefkens, van 59. Asen gheplant.	1015.
Een Viseroy, van 658. Asen gheplant.	4200.
De Monastier, van 542. Asen geplant.	920.
Een vroeghe Blijen-burgher, van 171. Asen gheplant.	900.
Een Gouda, van 244. Asen gheplant.	1500.
Een Tulpa Kos, van 485. Asen geplant.	305.
Een Butterman (schoon) van 246. Asen gheplant.	250.
Een wit Purper Ieroen, van 148. Asen gheplant.	475.
Een Parragon van Delft of Mols-wijck, van 123. Asen gheplant.	500.
Een Aanvers Vestus, van 52. Asen geplant.	510.
Een Sjery Katelijn, vande beste 300zt/ van 619. Asen gheplant.	2610.
Een Ameraal van der Eyk, van 446. Asen gheplant.	1620.
Een Grebber, van 95. Asen geplant.	615.
Een Gouda, van 156. Asen geplant.	1165.
Een Tulpa Kos, van 117. Asen geplant.	205.
Een Parragon Schilder, van 106. Asen gheplant.	1615.
Een Laroy, van 306. Asen geplant.	510.
Een Sjery na by, van 129. Asen geplant.	755.
Een Fama, van 158. Asen geplant.	700.
Een Fama, van 130. Asen geplant.	605.
Een Af-zet van Sjery Katelijn, van 206. Asen gheplant.	1280.
Een Somer-Schoon, van 368. Asen geplant.	1010.
Een Amerael vander Eyk, van 214. Asen gheplant.	1045.
Een Parragon Kasteleyn, van 100. Asen gheplant.	450.
Een Gouda, van 125. Asen geplant.	1015.
Een Amerael Katelijn, van 181. Asen gheplant.	225.
Een ghevlamde Iacot, van 100. Asen gheplant.	94.
Een Wit-Purper van Buscher, van 134. Asen gheplant.	110.
Een Wit-Purper van Buscher, van 315. Asen gheplant.	245.
Een Wit-Purper van Buscher, van 481.	

Een swymende Ian Gerritsz. van 925. Asen geplant.	210.
Een swymende Ian Gerritsz. van 80. Asen geplant.	51.
Een Bruyne Blaeuwe Purper van Kouper, van 790. Asen geplant.	220.
Een Lantmeter, van 277. Asen geplant.	365.
Een Lantmeter, van 71. Asen geplant.	175.
Een Parragon de Man, van 148. Asen geplant.	260.
Een Bruyne Lack vander Meer, van 365. Asen gheplant.	215.
Een Amerael vander Eyck, van 92. Asen gheplant.	510.
Een Fama, van 104. Asen geplant.	440.
Een Brabanson Bol, van 524. Asen geplant.	975.
Een Grebber, van 523. Asen gheplant.	1485.
Een Brabanson, van 542. Asen geplant.	1010.
Een Brabanson, van 346. Asen geplant.	835.
Een Schapesteyn, van 95. Asen geplant.	235.
Een Gouda, van 160. Asen geplant.	1165.
Een Gouda, van 82. Asen geplant.	765.
Een Gouda, van 63. Asen geplant.	635.

Dese naevolghende Perceelen zijn by de Aes verkocht/ ende te leveren als de Bollen acht daghen uyt der Aerden sijn ghewecst.

Inden eersten 1000. Asen Groote Gepluymezeerde.	280.
Noch 1000. Asen Legrandes.	780.
Noch 1000. Asen Vyolette Gevlamde Rottgansen.	805.
Noch 1000. Asen Aenversen, vande ghemeene soozt.	930.
Noch 1000. Asen Aenversen.	905.
Noch 1000. Asen Lanoijs.	500.
Noch 1000. Asen Zay-Blommen vande Kasteleyn, vande beste soozt.	1000.
Noch 500. Asen Lak van Rijn.	160.
Noch 1000. Asen Saij-Blommen, vande gemeene soozt.	495.
Noch 1000. Asen Nieu-Burgers	430.
Noch 500. Asen Nieu-Burgers	235.
Noch 1000. Asen Ian Symonsz.	140.
Noch 500. Asen Ian Symonsz.	70.
Noch 1000. Asen Mackx	300.
Noch 1000. Asen Mackx	300.
Noch 1000. Asen Recktors	310.
Noch 1000. Asen Vyolette ghevlamde Rotgansen.	725.
Noch 500. Asen Vyolette ghevlamde Rotgansen.	375.
Noch 1000. Asen Late Blyen-Burgers.	570.
Noch 1000. Asen Ducke-winckel.	210.
Noch 1000. Asen Petters.	730.
Noch 1000. Asen Wt-roep.	705.
Noch 1000. Asen Wt-roep.	725.
Noch 1000. Asen Petters.	705.
Noch 1000. Asen Tornay Kasteleyn.	705.
Noch 1000. Asen Tornay Rijkers.	345.
Noch 500. Asen gevlamde Bransons de	

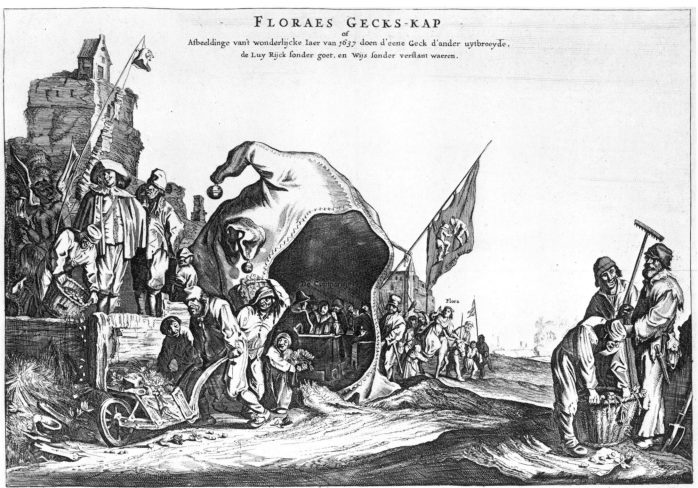

patterns (or "breaks") were not stable and would change from one tulip generation to the next. Horticulturists of the period thus decided to create an imaginary "ideal" tulip against which all other tulips could be measured. The degree to which a real tulip deviated from the ideal dictated its quality. The highest grade was labeled "super fine"; a tulip that laid claim to this distinction was permitted to show only a trace of the parent bulb's original color. If, for example, the parent bulb was pink and its offspring white with a thin band of pink around the base, it was awarded the "super fine" grade. The finer a tulip, the higher a price it fetched at bulb auctions. The object was to have as "fine" a tulip as possible—but how? That was the problem, because the principle of color mutation was not understood.

The historian Nicolaas van Wassenaar thought he had the solution to this problem—he reported that the Syrians were able to change the color of a tulip by transplanting it. He noted that tulips grown in Holland had colors that differed from the parent bulbs originating in other countries and climates. Had he pursued this, he might have discovered the real cause of mutations.

Experiments were carried out in the hope of producing multicolored flowers. Two halves of two different bulbs were attached to each other, though with little success. (This method was used successfully much later in England.) Horticulturists also discovered that the presence of lice in tulip beds caused mutations. It was not realized at the time, but with this discovery, horticulturists had come very close to discovering the cause of breaks: transmission of a virus by

opposite: Another caricature of the wind trade, this time symbolized by an oversized fool's cap. The caption reads: "Picture of the wonderous year 1637 when fools made fools of each other, when the rich were penniless, and when scholars were stupid." The engraving is by Pieter Nolpe.

There are tulips that hardly change from one century to the next. Compare this 17th-century tulip painting by Judith Leyster (*right*) with the photograph of a very similar modern variety (*above*).

insects. But what did a 17th-century horticulturist know about viruses?

In an 18th-century tulip book, the horticulturist D. H. Cause stated: "Experience has shown that a poor bulb produces a flower more beautiful than before and then immediately dies, as if it has used its last strength to please its owner."

Cause was correct in his observations—the beauty of such flowers was a beauty of death. The prettier a flower, the closer it was to dying out. The reason for this—and its cure—would wait centuries for discovery.

Tulipomania or the Wind Trade

The fascination with the tulip, its endless mutations and mystery, gave it immense value. Here was a product so costly that it was literally worth its weight in gold. Yet the bulb was so unattractive that given a chance to steal it, a thief would probably pass it by. All one had to do to become rich was to put it into the ground and wait. Its potential as an investment was being discovered. But it wasn't only wealth that spurred the tulip traders on, for they were already among the wealthiest citizens of the country. They were seeking something else, a new status symbol, new ways to flaunt their wealth and position. They all had gardens at their summer residences that resembled the Garden of Eden, realms replete with fountains, rare plants, scale models of Greek temples, marble statues, aviaries with rare birds from far away places. How could they possibly hope to outdo each other? The

ACCURATE DESCRIPTION
of the Whole Collection of FINE
HYACINTHS,
TULIPS
AND
RANONCULUSES;
That are Collected from the different
Dutch Flowrift's, and to gether
to be found in the Large
dutch Flowergarden from
VOORHELM and SCHNEEVOOGT,
Flowrifts and feedsmen at Haerlem in Holland,
Which Direction was formerly V o o r-
h e l m and van Z o m p e l.

H A E R L E M,

Printed for the Authors, by whom it is to be
had *Gratis* to Every Curious Man.

almighty bulb was the answer. How satisfying it must have been to take one's guests out into the garden, knowing full well that *they* understood the value of the flowers and knew that your rare bulbs were not to be had for love or money.

The middle and lower-middle classes were aware of the value placed on the tulip by the higher classes, and many of them thought that they, too, would have a chance to become rich. They reasoned that if experienced businessmen could spend such large sums for a silly, little tulip bulb—and make a profit—then it must be a good business opportunity. Small businesses were sold and the money invested in bulbs. A wave of speculation ensued. No one could resist the tulip's gaming tables.

As a result of the rise in prices caused by speculation, tulips were no longer sold by quantity, but by weight. The unit of measurement used was the *aas* (0.048 grams); 20 *aasen* were equivalent to about 1 gram. Bulbs were usually sold while they were still planted, and the weight had to be estimated. The buyer would often sell the bulbs at a profit to a third party; the third party would in turn sell them to a fourth, at a profit; and so on. And all of these transactions occurred without anyone's actually seeing the bulbs involved.

It was trading in something as elusive, as insubstantial, as the wind—and it did in time come to be called the "wind trade"—and sometimes "tulipomania" (see pages 44, 46, 48, 52, 53). Many a person threw himself into it with reckless abandon, showing no concern for his future. For the moment, the successes were too tempting; who could

51

left and opposite above: Broken tulips were popular until well into the 19th century. The famous Zomerschoon, shown here in an illustration dating from 1794, is still grown in small numbers and is considered the showpiece of the "broken" tulips.

below: Jan Brueghel II (1601–78) used monkeys to depict the folly of tulipomania. The group of monkeys on the veranda was meant to ridicule the tulip brokers' penchant for rich food and drink.

These bills of lading give an idea of the extent of the Dutch bulb export industry during the 19th century. They were for shipments destined for Frankfurt (1815), Lübeck (1816), and New York (1830). Notable in these bills is the invocation of the Lord's protection for the ship and her crew. The document is sent "in the name of God and under his protective care." According to the bill of lading, the ship's captain and God are cocaptains and the captain promises to "sail with the first good wind that God shall grant" and to deliver his cargo "should God grant me a safe voyage." It concludes with the words "Ordained by God."

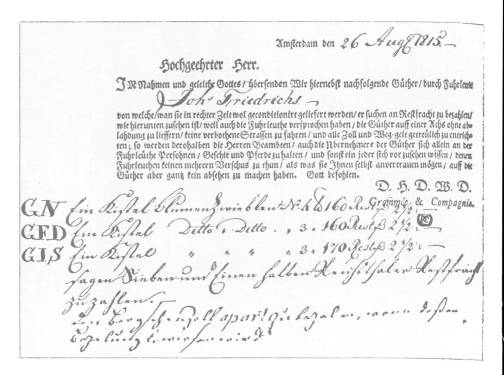

resist the chance to earn 60,000 florins ($44,000) in a month? This is a fortune by any standard.

The Dutchmen who were really better off for all this were the innkeepers, for it was in their establishments that many of the speculative transactions were carried out. The traders spent days and nights at the inns, eating and drinking the expensive foods paid for with their profits.

However vehemently ministers preached from the pulpits against the evils of this "moral decline," no matter how often the speculators were ridiculed in print, they continued to go about the business of buying and selling bulbs. They continued even when the already exhorbitant prices increased at dizzying rates. If a buyer did not have money to pay for his deals, he was prepared to give away his belongings. It is reported that five pounds of 'Yellow Crown' tulips were sold for 1875 florins, but the buyer could only come up with 500 florins in cash. The balance was paid for with a horse and calèche. Another tulip merchant asked for "a sideboard of ebony decorated with many mirrors and a large painting of flowers" plus cash for a bulb. He got his price. Another deal was sealed with the payment of a new carriage with two dapple-gray horses, a sleigh with yet another horse, a painting of Judas, and a painting by Ruysdael.

There were no limits to the excesses of those days. Municipal governments tried to pass laws against bulb speculation, but without success, and it became increasingly apparent that it would have to end in disaster.

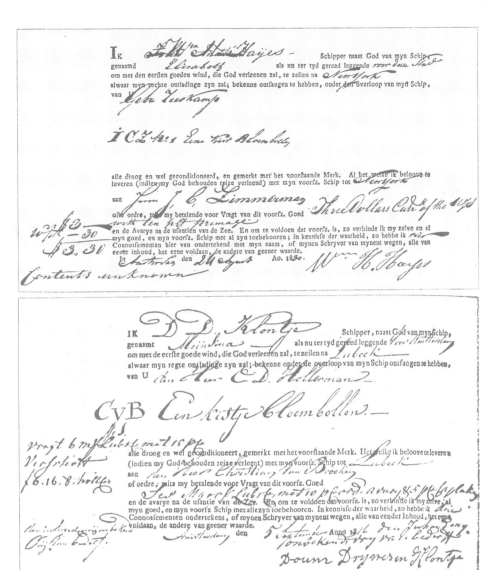

The end finally came on February 3, 1637, at an inn where a number of mechants were buying and selling bulbs. It was the general consensus of those at the meeting that there was something amiss. They decided to test the market prices and began by offering a pound of 'Crown' tulips for sale; the person who bought them would be paid a premium of a *Rijksdalder* (2½ florins). Someone immediately offered 1250 florins and the bidding stopped. The merchants thought that this had happened too quickly, and decided to carry out the experiment a second time, this time with a double premium. But on the second round, only 1100 florins were offered. A third attempt followed, but with less than 1000 florins being offered. Those present realized that bulb prices were artificial and did not reflect their actual value. The bottom had fallen out of the market.

Word spread quickly. An auction held two days later in Alkmaar was not affected by the developments of two days earlier, and prices there were as high as ever (see page 47). Bulb merchants throughout the country soon sent representatives to a meeting in Utrecht called to discuss the situation and to establish measures that would reverse the downward slide of bulb prices. The list of the towns represented shows just how far-reaching the consequences of the February 3 meeting were: Haarlem, Delft, Leiden, Alkmaar, Amsterdam, Gouda, Utrecht, Enkhuizen, Medemblik, De Streek in West Friesland, and Vianen, the sanctuary for the bankrupt who wished to hide from their creditors.

The meeting was unsuccessful. Measures against speculation had been instituted only by the municipal government of Haarlem, and

Many artists, especially Dutch artists
during the 17th and 18th centuries, were
captivated by the color and shape of the
tulip. The two small paintings to the far
right are by J. Marrel. The larger
illustration of three tulips is by H.
Henstenburgh. To the right is an example
of work by H. G. Knip and in the bottom
left hand corner of this page, a watercolor
by Maria Sibylla Merian.

1811.

ACTE van PATENT.

Departement van de Zuiderzee,

N°. *30.*   H A A R L E M.

DE MAIRE der Stad HAARLEM, gezien hebbende de aanvrage van
E. H. Krelage

wonende binnen deze Stad, Wijk *j A* N°. *97.* , zich hebbende aangegeven als
Bloemist.

en van mij gevraagd Patent tot de uitoeffening van voornoemd Bedrijf, voor den tijd van twaalf Maanden, ingaande den *10e April 1811*, en zullende eindigen den *10e April 1812* Wintermaand 1811; heb ik, vermits mij geen redenen ter contrarie zijn voorgekomen, de Acte tot uitoeffening van voormeld Bedrijf, ingevolge de Ordonnantie op het Regt van Patent in dato 2 van Wintermaand 1805, aan denzelven afgegeven, om te strekken daar en zoo het behoord; met verzoek aan elk en een iegelijk, wien zulks zoude mogen aangaan, denzelven als zoodanig te erkennen, en het effect der voornoemde Ordonnantie te doen en te laten genieten, mits zich onderwerpende aan en gedragende naar de Wetten van de exterende Reglementen van Policie.
HAARLEM den *10e van Louwmaand* 1811.

Handteekening van den Gepatenteerde.   *Op last van de Maire bovengemeld,*

Solvit Zegel *ƒ 1. 8.*
Stads Belasting *2. 12.*
Leges *7.*
ƒ 6. 19. 8.
Goed tot den *10e April* 1812.

NOTA: *Deze Acte van Patent zal bij Overlijden of quitering der affaire ter Griffie moeten worden terug bezorgt.*

left: During Holland's occupation by French troops, all those who wished to operate a business were required to obtain a *patent* (license) from the *maire* (mayor) of the town in which he lived. The *patent* shown here is the one issued to E. H. Krelage, one of the pioneers of the Dutch bulb industry.

below: This detail of a larger map shows just how many bulb companies had established themselves in a small section of Haarlem in 1806. Block 53 is the nursery of the Zwanenburg (Van Tubergen) Firm, the only one still in existence.

little had changed officially for those who wished to continue their old business practices, despite recent developments.

Various cities pleaded with the central government, the States of Holland, to implement measures against speculation. The States in turn asked the Courts for an opinion. Two days later, on April 27, 1637, the States decided to leave the matter up to the cities themselves. Those ruined by the end of the wind trade would for many years suffer the consequences of their greed. They were forced to build up their lives again from scratch. However, the tragic conclusion to this chapter of the tulip's history did not lessen interest in the flower as an object of beauty and grace.

Tulips Invade the World

Despite the rise and fall of the tulip in The Netherlands, it continued to enjoy prominence elsewhere in 17th- and 18th-century Europe. At the court of Louis XIV, France's "Sun King," the tulip was, as previously mentioned, the court flower *par excellence.* Parisian bulb growers were in direct contact with their counterparts in Rijssel, Belgium, and Valencin (see above and page 50). In 1616 the popular printmaker Chrispijn van de Passe spent most of the year in Paris, where he produced a number of tulip prints that were acclaimed for their beauty.

Tulips bloomed in the famous gardens of other European Courts: the Zwinger in Dresden, the Residenz in Wurzburg, the Lustgarten in Berlin, Schönbrunn in Vienna, Mirabelle in Salzburg, Nymphenburg

right: As early as the 19th century, bulb dealers made use of standard catalogues in four languages; they could have the name and address of their own firm printed on the cover.

below: Flower exhibitions increased in popularity during the 19th century. The second exhibition organized by the Dutch Bulb Society in Haarlem (1862), shown here in a contemporary print, was a great success.

GRAND CATALOGUE DES PLUS BEAUX

O I G N O N S

ET PATTES à FLEURS HOLLANDAISES

comme des

HACINTHES, TULIPES, RENONCULES, ANEMONES.

et toutes autres Sortes de Fleurs,

qui se vendent, chez

VAN OUKERKE en VAN EMMERIK,

Fleuristes à Harlem en Hollande, dans le Ruilenburgerlaan, Q. 4. No. 81.

CATALOGUE of FLOWERROOTS,

AND BULBS

to besold bii

VAN OUKERKE en VAN EMMERIK,

Florities at Harlem in Holland, in the Ruilenburgerlaan, Q. 4. No. 81.

GROSSER CATALOGUS

von Holländischen

BLUMEN ZWIEBELN, und WURZELN,

welche zu haben sind bey der Blumist

VAN OUKERKE en VAN EMMERIK,

Blumisten bij Haarlem in Holland, in de Ruilenburgerlaan, Q. 4. No. 81.

GROOTE HOLLANDSCHE CATALOGUS

van de Allervoortreffelijkste

BOL- EN WORTEL - BLOEMEN,

die te bekomen zijn bij

VAN OUKERKE en VAN EMMERIK,

Bloemisten te Haarlem in Holland, in de Ruilenburgerlaan, Q. 4. No. 81.

in Munich, and Saint-Cloud and Versailles in France. Painters everywhere were inspired by the tulip, and such royal ladies as Maria-Theresa of Austria, Leopoldine, Empress of Brazil, Marie-Antoinette and Empress Joséphine of France became patrons of the arts.

The dramatic events of the final decade of the 18th and the first half of the 19th centuries—the French Revolution and Napoleon's invasion and occupation of The Netherlands—brought to an end the period of lightheaded folly in which Queen Tulipa reigned. Once this had happened, the way was paved for a more sober approach to the tulip and to its commercial appeal.

In the 19th century, bulb flowers, for the most part hyacinths, grew in profusion in the area around Berlin—in such quantities that at one point, a million and a half hyacinths were exported to Holland. Rombach records that the "tulip kings along the Spree ride in their own coaches and all wear high hats." A flower show held in Berlin in 1840 was so popular and so well attended that the organizers could not keep track of the number of visitors and just threw the admission receipts into a large box.

Eventually, however, this all came to an end. Berlin was a rapidly expanding city, and the land occupied by bulb flowers was needed for building. Berlin's reputation as a city of flowers soon declined.

The tulip was given special prominence at the 1843 International Flower Show held in Paris. Among the entries was that of Monsieur Tripet, with over 800 tulip varieties; the entry was awarded a gold

medal by the Countess d'Orléans. Tulip growers in Lille, however, suspected that Tripet's tulips were not of the highest quality and that *their* tulips should have received the prize. They called in a panel of experts to arbitrate the matter, but when the judges sided with the Parisian judges, the Lille growers protested. Disgusted with the whole affair, the judges refused to consider any more entries, with the result that it was a number of years before flower competitions were again held in France. The Lille growers, however, were extremely competent horticulturists, and throughout the 19th century, their bulbs commanded the highest prices.

The Belgian growers contributed to the development of the Darwin varieties, albeit in an indirect way. By the late 19th century, all but one of the famous Flemish tulip collections had disappeared. The one that remained, that of Lenglart, was put up for sale because its owner was too elderly to continue to care for it. The Haarlem grower J. H. Krelage purchased the Lenglart collection because he saw that the monochromed, breeder tulips that it contained would serve as the foundation of a new type of tulip. He was able to develop just such a new class—the popular Darwins found in gardens and parks around the world.

The tulip has, of course, enjoyed much success and popularity in other countries. The English have been interested in tulips almost as long as have the Dutch (see page 45). There have even been some interesting parallels between the Dutch and the English in this respect. In 17th-century England it was the broken and feathered

The first scientific studies of tulips, daffodils, amaryllis, and irises in modern times were carried out under the direction of Professor A. H. Blaauw (1882–1942), a noted plant physiologist *(below)*. He attempted to discover the growth cycles of bulb plants. The drawings to the left show such cycles for tulip bulbs and were produced by R. Mulder and Ida Luyten in 1928. These illustrations are from one of the most imporant works on tulips. Under Professor Blaauw's direction, an important series of publications were issued that stimulated the growth and development of the bulb industry.

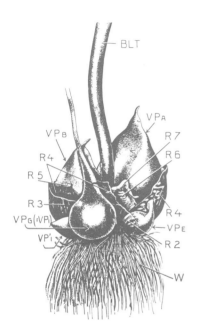
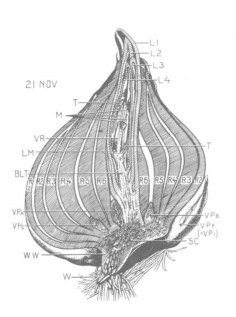

tulips that achieved the greatest popularity; and as late as 1843 exhorbitant prices were being asked for some varieties.

There were at one time two tulip clubs in England, one in the northern part of the country and one in the southern. Each club had established its own standards of excellence: one looked only at the shape of the flower and not at its color; the other club took exactly the opposite view. Tulips were put on display at exhibitions with only their petals exposed, the stem and leaves being hidden beneath a wooden board. Tulips, the English thought, had to be shaped like a half-sphere. If, for example, a tulip were placed into a half of a tennis ball, it would have to fit like a glove.

The tulip first gained popularity in England among the working classes of the Midlands region and not, as on the Continent, among the rich and powerful. Tom Stores, one of England's most famous tulip experts, was a railroad engineer who grew his tulips alongside the railroad tracks.

The National Tulip Society in England was active until the 1930s when, for a number of reasons, its activities were curtailed. Attempts have recently been made to revive the society, and interest is once again on the rise.

There is a basic difference, however, between the Dutch and the British when it comes to tulips. For many years—perhaps too many—the English have looked upon the tulip only as a hobby rather than as a serious commercial enterprise. This attitude was reflected in their fondness for mutant tulips long after it was recognized that these were

The Laboratory for Bulb Research in Wageningen, where Professor Blaauw and his colleagues carried out their work.

the result of viral infections. The amateurish goal of raising half-spherical tulips was also a sign of this, as was the battle that Krelage had with his English counterparts over the status of the Darwin tulips.

However, the British have achieved results equal to those of the Dutch growers. The flower gardens of Spalding, Lincolnshire, have been called the "English Keukenhof." Spalding is also the scene of an annual tulip festival that the Dutchman Jos van Driel had a part in starting. These activities have been largely stimulated by a gradual increase in the commercial exploitation of the tulip in Great Britain.

Few people, however, are as devoted today to the tulip as are the Dutch. The flower is available in Holland at any flower shop for a reasonable price (see page 11). Recently, department stores and supermarkets have begun to enter the flower market in the hope of providing their clients with "one-stop shopping." The growers and exporters make catalogues available to their customers with up-to-date information on the availability of tulip varieties. This practice dates back to the 17th century, when price lists were printed in small quantities, and always on light blue paper.

Beginning in 1818, a series of flower shows in Holland gave the public the spectacular exhibits they had not seen for years. There were no prizes awarded at these shows, for as one Haarlem grower editorialized in a newspaper at the time, "We don't want to risk our tulips' losing to an outsider's flowers, which are, of course, of vastly inferior quality." This fear was soon laid to rest, and expositions were held with increasing frequency. The Haarlem grower Krelage had

Greigii tulips are among the most extraordinary kinds of tulip known. Eduard August Regel referred to the Greigii as the "Queen of Tulips" in his 1873 work, *Gartenflora*. In 1872 he received a shipment of Greigii bulbs from Russia and planted half of them indoors and half outdoors. Only those planted outdoors bloomed. Note the purple spots on the leaves, a characteristic unique in the world of tulips.

In the early part of the 20th century, the Dutch growers attempted to bring their product to other parts of the world. They once offered enough tulip bulbs to fill the Tuileries Gardens in Paris. The French government accepted the offer, and along with the bulbs came a Dutch couple—complete with their Volendam costumes.

created a winter garden that attracted a constant stream of visitors, including royalty.

More and more today there are very different kinds of kings and especially queens: the Butter Queen, the Cheese Queen, and, of course, the Tulip Queen. A Tulip Queen is elected annually in the city of Holland, Michigan, a town with a large population of Dutch ancestry. This city was originally a settlement formed by members of the Dutch Reformed church who fled Holland during persecution under King Willem I (1813–40). They left Holland, much as did the Pilgrim Fathers before them, to make a new life in America. The voyage was difficult, and many did not survive the crossing. But with the Reverend Van Raalte as their leader, they established themselves on the prairies of Michigan. This "Little Holland" is now a flourishing city, and although completely Americanized, it does not forget its Dutch roots. Each year a Tulip Festival is held there—an occasion for parades, Dutch costumes, bands, and fairs.

Pella, Iowa, has a big tulip festival every year, and so does Orange City, Iowa, Albany, New York, and many other locations in America where the city founders were Dutch. The group of Netherlanders who founded Pella had chosen the town's name before they left home. It means "City of Refuge."

The dates of these festivals and the activities included are similar. The second week in May produces a fine display of color, and the weather is apt to be favorable for outdoor events; so, that is the chosen time. There is usually a tulip show taking place throughout the

Tulip season is the occasion for festivities the world over. One of the most famous events is the Canadian Tulip Festival, during which thousands of bulbs bloom in the gardens of the Dominions's Parliament Buildings in Ottawa.

festival's duration; a queen is chosen and crowned; a children's fair is held, complete with costumes and prizes; and sometimes a festival ball brings the holiday to its conclusion. In Albany the festival is opened by a ceremony called the "Scrubbing of State Street" by Dutch-costumed members of the City Club of Albany, Inc., and a similar ceremony is carried out in some of the other festivals.

Canada's capital city, Ottawa, claims the honor of having the largest public display of tulips in North America, and a few years ago that display included over three million tulip blossoms of 200 varieties. From the time the Ottawa Improvement Commission was formed (1899), the city paid great attention to its public gardens, but it was due to the close ties with the Dutch during World War II that the emphasis swung over to tulips. Queen Juliana (Crown Princess at that time) spent part of the war years in Canada and gave birth to a daughter in the Ottawa Civic Hospital—a spot that was declared Dutch soil so that the child would be born a Dutch national. In 1945, as a personal "thank you" from Queen Juliana for Canada's hospitality, and as a public "thank you" to the soldiers of Canada who helped to free Holland, Ottawa was given 100,000 tulip bulbs. Every year since then more bulbs have come from the grateful Dutch people, as well as from other donors, and now the city is known far and wide for its tulip display. Since 1951 Ottawa has held an annual Spring Festival in the middle of May, with parades, regattas, fireworks, and an amateur photographic contest, as well as international food and craft fairs. In the midst of the variety of these activities, however, the tulip reigns supreme.

3 Growers, Exporters, Merchants

The picture on the left shows the method formerly employed to spread liquid fertilizer over the bulb fields. This required much skill, strong arms, and a cooperative wind. Hydraulic engineering is an important part of bulb growing. The fields cannot be too moist, yet there must be an adequate water supply. The picture at the center shows preparations being made for the installation of a new irrigation system.

When Henrick Van der Schoot landed at the port of Hellevoestsluis on the Dutch coast on October 5, 1849, having just spent the better part of a year traveling through the United States to sell the tulip bulb to America, he could not have imagined that 100 years later his travels would be known as the maiden voyage of the Dutch bulb export industry. Thanks to his diary, we have a record of his travels—the places he visited, the number of miles logged, the exact expenses incurred. He began his trip in early March, 1849, and traveled through the United States until August 29, when his ship, the *Serapis* —a windjammer—set sail for Holland. The journey was not a comfortable one, according to Van der Schoot's diary: "The ship rolls violently from side to side—high seas ahead—terrifying northwesterly winds—seas that reach to the heavens."

Van der Schoot was only one of hundreds who eventually traveled to sing the praises of the tulip. Bulb merchants visited Germany, England, Scandinavia, the Balkans, France, Italy, and Russia in their search for markets (see page 59). In those days, travel meant hardships and deprivation. A trip from New York to Rotterdam lasted at least six weeks and a business trip to America meant being away from home for at least six months.

Once the travelers returned to Holland with their order books filled, there was no time for rest; bulbs had to be harvested, peeled, counted, packed, and shipped back to the countries from which the salesmen had just come. Their wives took care of the home, raised the children, and often looked after the business as well.

It is said in the bulb region that spading is hard work, yet viewing here from a slightly elevated angle, *(below right)* one would almost say that it is the work of an artist. These days, this preparation of the fields is almost always done by machine. A simple, hand-operated device *(below left)* makes grooves in the tulip bed into which bulbs will later be placed. An alternative to this two-man device is the one that can be used by one man *(opposite above)*. The large photograph *(opposite below)* shows the grooves, which are being filled with bulbs. While these manual operations are a thing of the past, they illustrate how laborious the bulb industry was in former days.

Many exporters took great risks in getting their bulbs abroad during time of war. One man, who wanted to beat his competition, actually tried to sail to the United States by himself, an attempt that led to his being torpedoed. As his ship was going down, however, he managed to save himself and one thing: his price lists! When he finally did make it to the United States, he made sure that his clients knew of his adventure, which won him many new American customers.

Persistence and a creative approach to marketing (one young exporter succeeded in persuading the manager of an American shoe store to buy tulip bulbs for gifts to his customers) helped the Dutch merchants to expand the market abroad. However, the men who went to Russia in 1917 found themselves in the midst of a revolution. One Dutchman, trapped at the outbreak of the Russian uprising, managed to escape with a refugee, whom he later married. As a result, he was known in Holland for many years thereafter as "the Russian." Another tulip merchant managed to travel to Petrograd in 1917 to see if there were still business opportunities to be exploited. He spent seven months as a diplomatic courier, commuting between Saint Petersberg (now Leningrad) and Moscow, where he made the acquaintance of the Soviet Minister of Foreign Affairs. When he finally returned to his homeland, he carried only official documents from the Royal Netherlands Embassy in Moscow; there were no orders for tulip bulbs to be had in Soviet Russia.

Wars interrupted this routine of travel and work, even though the Dutch did their best to continue shipments on a regular basis. During

World War I, for example, a shipment of bulbs was scheduled for transport to the United States on the Holland-America Line's *New Amsterdam*. The ship sailed as scheduled, but was forced to turn back because the outer harbor had been mined. The bulbs were transferred to the *Amsteldijk*, but it was months later before the ship could safely set sail. Another shipment rotted after sitting for months in the ship's hold during a heat wave. Heat was a problem that plagued the bulb industry until the invention of "containers," which could be loaded on the bulb firm's own premises and transported to the ship at the last minute.

The Tulip Boom

The end of conflicts in Europe marked the beginning of a surge in trade. On November 11, 1918, the day that marked the end of World War I, the Dutch shipped 12 million kilos (13,200 tons) of bulbs. Ten years later, this amount had almost quadrupled—42 million kilos (46,000 tons). These years of prosperity, however, did not continue. First came the financial crisis of 1929 and then, after a brief respite, German aggression in Europe and the outbreak of World War II with all its devastations.

After the liberation of Holland in 1945, the Dutch set about the task of rebuilding their bulb industry with the slogan: "On to a hundred million guilders!" This was more than double the amount of exports, even in the best of years, prior to the war, and, before long, annual

opposite: As winter approaches, the bulb fields are strewn with hay to protect the bulbs from cold and frost. Passing through the bulb region on a late fall day, one sees haystacks dotting the landscape, readied for the winter ahead.

below: The photograph joins the past with the present. This field was once a sand dune, parts of which can be seen in the background. But as sand was needed for the construction of new buildings in Amsterdam, the dunes were gradually reduced until a flat field remained.

exports exceeded not 100 but 500 million guilders. The industry was given a shot in the arm by the appointment of Professor E. van Slogteren as Director of the Dutch Laboratory for Bulb Research, and under his guidance, the Dutch bulb industry flourished to a previously unimaginable degree.

The increase in exports came about, of course, with a proportional increase in production, and these developments led to an abrupt change in relationships between the grower and the exporter. Many exporters, then as now, grew their own bulbs; but when they could not produce enough to meet demands, they were forced to purchase bulbs elsewhere. Around the turn of the century, this was done on the basis of a complicated system of long-term credit and loans.

If a grower wished to receive payment before November 1 for bulbs delivered earlier in the year, he had to pay the interest on his own loan to the exporter. This arrangement was hardly in the best interests of the grower, but helped strengthen the exporter's position. He was required to pay his creditors only when and if his customers paid for their shipments. If a customer faulted on an invoice, it was unfortunate for the exporter, but even more so for the grower: the exporter lost relatively little, the grower everything. This way of buying and selling bulbs for export meant that one needed only a small amount of working capital to set up an export company. Industrious men who were willing to work for their wage were given the opportunity to set themselves up as their own bosses. It was the dream of every bulb grower to have his own export firm.

The Royal Dutch Bulb Society

Eventually, though, the growers realized that this system of credits was not to their best advantage—that it was limiting *their* growth—and so they organized themselves into the Dutch Bulb Society (later to become the Royal Dutch Bulb Society). The Society established a system of auctions, a code of ethics, and a court of arbitration to settle disputes. Auctions gave growers an insight into the world of business and prices. When competition arose between grower and exporter, prices dropped, forcing both sides to operate on extremely narrow profit margins.

The bulb industry, today worth millions in exports, revolves around one thing and one thing only: the success or failure of the bulb crop. Without a successful crop, the bulb industry would suffer a serious setback because bulbs cannot be "stockpiled" from year to year as can, say, wheat or corn. But because the bulb industry in Holland *is* an entire industry, it can survive and hold its monopoly on the sale of bulbs throughout the world. Holland is the only country in this position, even though there are other places in the world where bulbs are grown successfully.

The bulb producer's life is centered on his product, attuned to its growth cycles. Planting (see pages 68, 69), harvesting (see page 74), selling and shipping (see page 75) are the stages of the bulb's path from the field to the customer, and this sets the rhythm of the grower's activities. Two expressions commonly heard in the bulb region show

below and opposite: Crossing two tulip varieties requires extreme patience and precision. Here the anthers of one variety are carefully removed and placed in a small plastic box. The chances for success are perhaps one in a thousand because the goal is not to produce just a new variety, but a more beautiful and stronger one. The hybridizer holds the box with anthers in one hand and, with a small brush, carefully removes the pollen. The pollen is then transferred to the ovary of the tulip selected for cross-breeding. The new varieties produced in this way are then subjected to a strict elimination procedure, and only the best are selected for propagation. It is in this way that the tulip assortment has been expanded.

the extent to which the bulb influences the growers' lives: *We hebben ze nog niet in de mand,* or "We don't have them in the basket yet" (roughly equivalent to, "Don't count your chickens before they're hatched"), and *We weten d'r met z'n allen niks van,* or "We don't really know anything about it."

The weather dictates whether the bulbs can be planted or harvested on time. If a growing season has been particularly rainy, the bulbs will rot in the warm, moist soil; unexpected frost or hail storms can destroy young tulips. Even the most conscientious grower can do little against such natural disasters.

Diseases and pests are the scourges of the bulb industry, and the grower must be constantly vigilant for their telltale signs. Wireworms, grubs, botrytis blight, bulb rot, and viral infections are but a few of the many threats with which growers must deal. Fortunately, the growers are assisted by government plant inspectors whose job it is to locate trouble spots before they can spread. These experts can often be seen walking through the bulb fields (on a sunny day, with a large black umbrella). For large fields, they often use a special cart to take them on their rounds. Their work is crucial to the survival of the Dutch bulb industry and to the safeguarding of its reputation as the source of high-quality bulbs and flowers. The work of the plant inspectors is backed up by the activities of the Laboratory for Bulb Research in Lisse.

The bulb is a unique product; that which the farmer grows (bulbs) is not what he sells (the promise of beautiful flowers *next* year). Once the

bulbs are packed in the fall, the bulb dealers, distributors, and exporters begin the task of shipping the bulbs to their destinations abroad or selling them through retailers in The Netherlands. No one, however, knows what the results will be the following spring, and this always has an effect on prices. Distributors and exporters often "cover" themselves by buying bulbs from several producers, thereby reducing the risk of their whole inventory being of poor quality. They bank on the hope that once the selling season gets underway, prices will rise as the quality of the flower bulbs becomes known.

The bulb grower himself is also subject to these same risks. He may have sold his bulbs at a low price when, in fact, it turns out to be a good year with high market prices. The opposite can also happen, in which case he can sit back and enjoy his success.

Grower and seller depend on each other for their livelihood. There is, however, a certain amount of tension between them, perhaps due to their close relationship—or *despite* their interdependence. Because there are no exact figures for the number of acres planted in a given year, nor of the yield of those acres, it is difficult to predict whether a given year will be "thick" or "thin." Those in whose interest it is to keep prices high spread the rumor that it has been a "bad year," that the bulbs in a particular area have all rotted, and those elsewhere are of poor quality. Distributors and exporters, of course, want to keep prices low and so spread the rumor that the market is flooded with bulbs, that the bottom will fall out of the market, and that foreign buyers do not seem to be buying in large quantities. This psychological

opposite: Clay bulbs are not planted as deep as other types, and it is therefore possible to harvest them by hand. Such a photograph is of historic value because the days when bulbs were harvested by hand are all but gone. It takes six years for a bulb flower grown from seed to reach maturity. The line drawings illustrate the six stages of development.

right: A barge passes peacefully down one of the many canals that once served as Holland's main means of transporting goods from one city to another.

left: One of the greatest of Holland's flower painters was Maria Sibylla Merian (1647–1717), who often included small creatures, such as butterflies and snails, as compositional and anecdotal accents.

left: These three judges are in the process of evaluating some of the many entries in the weekly flower show at the Hillegom Bulb Center.

right: The men are participating in a bulb auction. Each desk is equipped with a button; when pushed, a numbered light corresponding to the number of the desk lights up at the front of the auction hall.

opposite: In this way, the auction-goers can indicate their desire to purchase a particular lot. The one who is first to push his button is the one who buys it. The Hillegom Bulb Center also houses the Bulb Inspection Service, the Court of Arbitration for the Bulb Trade, and the Council of Dutch Bulb Merchants.

warfare does sometimes have an effect on prices, although which way it will go is really a matter of chance.

Wholesale bulb prices are published at regular intervals, and this gives a picture of price trends as the season progresses. But even this is not completely reliable. It is only late in the season that a shortage or an excess of bulbs becomes apparent. If there is a shortage, the prices can rise to such an extent that they actually affect the following year's market.

Rarely is there an entirely poor bulb crop. Where one bulb grower has a bad crop, a neighboring nursery may have a good one. If a particular variety is scarce in a given year, exporters will substitute another variety.

Through all this, bulbs are usually bought sight unseen, much as was the case during the tulipomania of the 17th century. This, of course, includes sales of bulbs that are still in the ground. If one visits the Hillegom weekly bulb auction on a Monday, not one bulb is found there (see above). Yet the man who buys "100,000 'Lustige Witwes,' size 12, harvested, dry, unblemished, unbroken skins" knows what he is buying. Sometimes special conditions are placed on the sale, depending on the country to which they are to be exported. For example, the United States Department of Agriculture and the United States Customs will not allow bulbs into the country if they show any trace of soil or sand—in case it carries the much-dreaded potato blight.

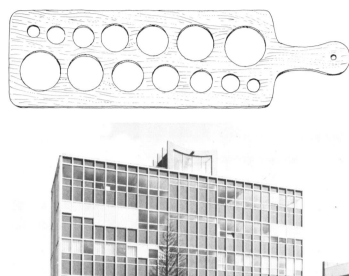

These days, bulbs are sorted for size mechanically. Once sorted, the bulbs are spot-checked with a hand-held measuring board such as the one shown below.

The Tulip Court

All bulb auctions and transactions are controlled by the Regulations for the Bulb Trade. Deals that were once concluded as gentlemen's agreements now are put into a written bill of sale—a good guarantee for maintaining friendships and avoiding misunderstandings. Good faith, however, is still part of the bulb man's code of ethics. Conflicts can arise, for example, when bulbs of the wrong variety are delivered—something that becomes known only the following spring— when the size or quantity of the shipment is not as agreed, or if the bulbs are unhealthy. Such matters can be referred for settlement to the Court of Arbitration for the Bulb Trade.

This court is composed of experienced professionals who draw on their own experience and personal knowledge of good and bad years. They understand the bulb's sensitivity to climate, disease, and pests— factors that often are at the heart of disputes. As a bulb grower or exporter himself, each member of the court has a practical knowledge of trade regulations and practices. He is chosen not only on the basis of his integrity, professional expertise, and impartiality, but also on his availability. The membership of the court changes to meet the needs of a particular case. A tulip expert, for example, would not be qualified to judge a case involving, say, dahlias or crocuses. The presiding officer and the court secretary are both lawyers. All members work as volunteers; the honor of sitting on the court is reward enough.

Bulb flowers make an excellent gift, both as cut flowers and as bulbs. It was the latter that the Dutch chose to present to the United States on the occasion of the Bicentennial in 1976. A parade *(right above)* marked the arrival of millions of bulbs in New York City. When the bulbs bloomed in the spring of 1976, they were a living advertisement for the Dutch bulb industry. Rome, Italy, has also received gifts of Dutch bulbs, as shown *(right below)* in a view of the park that surrounds the Colosseum.

left: Tulips blossom annually in the garden of New York City's Frick Collection.

When the tulips in the Cairo Botanical Gardens bloom each spring, they attract the attention of the public who are amazed to learn that tulips grow in their Middle Eastern country. The tulips shown here were presented by the Dutch to the Egyptian capital in 1976.

The costs involved in settling the dispute are usually the responsibility of the losing party, although in special cases both parties are required to share the responsibility. A small, struggling nursery can stand a chance of winning its dispute with a large, well-established export firm. Lawyers are rarely involved in the proceedings; and even if they were, chances are they would have little effect on the outcome. The court's decision is final and binding and has the same authority as a civil court. Those who do not comply with its decision are actually turned over to the bailiff or sheriff of the local civil court. The mere fact of the court's existence deters people from making deals that are less than honest. It is an old saying in Holland that "fighting over a cow ends up costing more than the cow." Because of the Court of Arbitration, however, this is not the case in the bulb industry.

The Dutch Auction

Bulbs can be sold directly to distributors by the growers themselves or through a middleman—who may be an independent agent—or the sales office of one of the various auction centers. Bulb auctions sell fewer bulbs than do the middlemen and distributors even though thousands of baskets of bulbs are traded in auction halls daily.

The first real indication of what kind of year it will be comes at the season's first bulb auction in June—not late in the season as one might expect. Only a few hundred baskets of bulbs may be offered for sale at this auction, yet the hall is usually filled to capacity. Each buyer takes

his place at a preassigned, numbered desk; each number corresponds to one on a large "clock" in the front of the hall (see pages 76, 77). The buyers sit with their fingers positioned anxiously on the button in front of them, and push it as soon as the auctioneer quotes a price they are willing to pay for the bulbs they want. If they are the first to respond to an offer, they have purchased the bulbs. (This is the origir of what is known in America as a "Dutch auction.") Should the first bid be too high, the buyers usually join in a chorus of whistles.

In earlier times, auctions were long, drawn-out sessions that often extended into the evening; these were known as "sandwich auctions" because the organizers would provide sandwiches and coffee for the buyers. Auction procedures have been streamlined so that today more bulbs can be sold in less time.

The so-called "green auction," a special event held in the bulb field itself, markets bulbs still in the ground. These auctions are usually held between March and May and are well-attended social functions. In the days when cars were rare, green auctions were even more popular. Buyers and sellers would gather in the early morning hours and spend the day doing business, chatting, and eating and drinking. Lunch was provided by the organizers of the auction. But as cars became more common, this practice was abandoned; people were able to go elsewhere to eat. Today one sees scores of cars parked along the roads that crisscross the bulb fields. The auction-goers crowd around the auctioneer: even from a distance, it is obvious what is going on.

INTERNATIONAL FLOWERSHOW·HOLLAND

FLORA

1953

HEEMSTEDE

14 MARCH-14 MAY

Single Early Tulips

Bloom in April
Height: 12 to 18 inches
This was the most popular class of tulips in the late 19th and the early 20th centuries. All Single Early tulips make excellent choices for gardens because they do not grow too high and they have strong stems.

1. Bellona
2. Brilliant Star
3. Couleur Cardinal
4. General de Wet
5. Prins Carnaval
6. Emperor's Crown (dates from 1750)
7. Princess Irene

Once the bulbs have been auctioned, bought, or sold, the work has just started, and the farmers and exporters need all the help they can get to keep this highly important industry prosperous. The Dutch government and many scientists and trade organizations help in this effort. Some of these have been mentioned earlier in this book, but their operation merits further attention.

Tulip Laboratories and Organizations

An important part of the bulb industry in Holland is the **Dutch Bulb Center,** located in the picturesque village of Hillegom. The main building of the center is flanked by gardens that contain many varieties of bulb and tuberous plants. The center is the scene of a weekly bulb auction and flower show. It also houses the **Royal Dutch Bulb Society,** the society's extensive library, the **Court of Arbitration for the Bulb Trade,** the **Bulb Inspection Service** (which works in cooperation with the Government Plant Inspection Service), and the **Council of Dutch Bulb Merchants.** The operations of the **Dutch Bulb Dealers' Association,** an organization of bulb exporters, is located in a nearby building.

The world-famous **Laboratory for Bulb Research** in Lisse is a unique institution, the activities of which complement those of the **Bulb Center in Hillegom.** More than half a century ago, those involved in the bulb trade saw the need for scientific investigation, not only to safeguard the bulb from disease and pests, but also to comply with the

5

6

7

often stringent regulations of foreign customs officials. When one looks at the laboratory's impressive buildings now, it is hard to imagine that this institution actually began in one room of the adjacent State Horticultural School. Soon the need for a new building was felt. The money for this purpose was raised by the growers themselves, but once the building was completed, the Dutch government assumed responsibility for managing it. The government, however, was unable to finance the insuring of the new building against fire and turned again to the growers and exporters to assume this expense. Their foresight paid off, for although the building burned down a few years later, it could be rebuilt almost immediately because of the insurance.

The activities of the laboratory have greatly expanded since those early days. New equipment and more staff have been added to meet the needs of modern scientific investigation—research on plant disease and pests, on new planting methods, on the effects of temperature on the bulb's growth cycles, and on many other problems. Both the grower and the exporter have benefited from this research.

The State Horticultural School located next door to the laboratory trains young people for careers as growers and exporters. They learn the basics of the industry and the practical aspects of running a bulb farm or exporting firm. Since many of the pupils come from agricultural or "bulb" families, what they learn here is the finishing touch to the practical experience that comes from working in the fields and seeing first hand what it means to raise bulbs. In fact, many bulb farmers continue in the profession of their fathers and grandfathers,

Double Early Tulips

Bloom in April
Height: 12 inches
Many of the varieties in this class of tulips
have been created through a crossing with
the rose Murillo. Because they are of the
same height and bloom at the same time,
they are particularly striking when grown in
combinations. They make excellent
additions to any flower bed.

1. Electra*
2. Orange Nassau*
3. Willemsoord*
4. Hytuna
5. Mr. Van der Hoer*
6. Peach Blossom*
7. Stockholm

   *Mutations of Murillo

although today's mechanized bulb farms are a far cry from those
operated with manual labor.

Despite their devotion to the flower, the number of families that
earn their living from bulb farming is decreasing. As the general
level of education increases from one generation to the next, young
people are drawn to the cities with the promise of better jobs or
perhaps a university education. While the bulb farmers may be the
backbone of the Dutch bulb industry, there are others who have also
made their contributions to the growth and success of this important
sector of Holland's economy.

The myth of the rich bulb farmer is, indeed, just a myth. Of course,
there are those who have managed to build up a good business; and
there are even those who live in spectacular homes along the edge of
bulb fields. But because most of these growers began modestly, such
accomplishments are all the more indicative of the hard work and
dedication that have gone into the development of the Dutch bulb
industry. In general, though, bulb growers lead a modest existence.
The size of their companies would rarely be classified as large—more
often than not, they are small, family-owned and family-operated
enterprises. Yet, despite this, production has increased at a
tremendous rate. The soil of the old Rhine delta is ideal for bulbs, and
this, coupled with improved methods, mechanization, and scientific
information about bulbs and their growing cycles, has been responsible
for much of the success of the industry.

Men of Tulips

Foremost on the list is **Dr. Ernst Heinrich Krelage,** one of the great family names of the Dutch bulb industry. A bust of Krelage's father stands in the entry hall of the Hillegom Bulb Center in recognition of his work in structuring the industry. The younger Krelage's doctoral dissertation, known affectionately in Holland as the "Bulb Bible," is still widely used as a valuable source of information on all aspects of bulbs.

While others may not have had the academic background of Dr. Krelage, their contributions are no less remarkable. **J. C. Janse** started his career in flowers as a sales clerk in the Wijs Seed Company of Amsterdam. He gradually acquired a reputation as an authority on both plants and insects. Janse maintained an extensive correspondence with foreign horticulturists as far away as Turkey. During his lifetime, he assembled a fantastic collection of rare plant books. His knowledge of bulb flowers was almost incredible. When he entered an exhibition hall, he could see at a glance which entries were outstanding and which were substandard. Although he died young, he was able to make a substantial contribution to the industry.

J. F. Ch. Dix began his career at the Krelage nursery in Haarlem, where he worked primarily with the development of hybrids. He did not limit himself to the tulip, however, and worked with many other bulb flowers as well. His reputation as a general horticulturist has

Double Late Tulips

Bloom in May
Height: 20 inches
Due to their large, heavy flowers, the stems
of this variety will often bend. Double Late
tulips should for this reason be planted in a
protected spot in the garden.

1. Gerbrand Kieft
2. Uncle Tom
3. Nizza

spread far and wide, partly as a result of his many publications. He has
served as a member of various professional committees and panels.

Tom M. Hoog was for many years codirector of the Van Tubergen
Bulb Company, the only combined bulb farm and export firm still in
operation in Haarlem. Van Tubergen himself was not by profession a
bulb man, although that is how he will be remembered. Hoog, too,
started out in life in a different profession, but went on to lead
expeditions to find the tulip's native habitat in Central Asia, China,
and Tibet. He and his colleagues were largely responsible for enriching
the tulip assortment with the ever-popular botanical (or species) tulips.
He was for many years Vice President of the governing board of the
Royal Dutch Bulb Society.

These men, and many more, have contributed immeasurably to the
growth and stability of the Dutch bulb industry. Scores of growers
have devoted their lives to hybridization, a long, tedious task that often
goes unrewarded. There are many who have made their contributions
behind the scenes—the managers of Keukenhof, organizers of flower
shows both in Holland and abroad, those who volunteer their time to
serve on commissions. All of these, regardless of their jobs, are "bulb
farmers" in the most general sense of the term.

Throughout all these developments, the Dutch government had
not until relatively recently kept pace with what was going on in the
bulb industry. Thousands of growers (who had at one time been helped
by government measures) and many export companies were being
bought up by foreign interests.

Mendel Tulips

Bloom in April
Height: 16 inches
These were the first long-stemmed tulips
grown in hothouses for sale as cut flowers.
They were developed around 1920 by E. H.
Krelage through a crossing between a Duc
van Tol and a Darwin tulip. These tulips
have in recent years become less popular,
Triumph tulips seem to have taken their
place. Shown here, Apricot Beauty.

Then the industry experienced a slump in the early 1970s when exports seemed to stagnate at about 450 million guilders annually. Something had to be done, and the government finally stepped in. One hundred thousand guilders were made available for a complete study of the Dutch bulb industry. The changes that resulted from this study were long-term ones that modified the structure of the industry.

Regardless of the situation within The Netherlands, the Dutch had to maintain their image of being *the* land of tulips—and sell that image to the world. The activities needed to do so were (and are) coordinated by the **Hillegom Bulb Center's promotional unit,** which has branch offices in New York, London, Bonn, Paris, Vienna, Zurich, Stockholm, and Milan. The Hillegom office promotes the entire Dutch bulb industry rather than the interests of a particular firm (see pages 79, 80). Customers (and potential customers) are provided with colorful, well-designed window displays, advertising copy, and folders with instructions for planting bulbs (which can, in turn, be given to retail customers). Although advertisements are placed in foreign newspapers occasionally, articles about Dutch bulbs in newspapers, gardening magazines, and trade journals are preferred. Radio and television are also used to promote the industry. And, of course, the work of the Bulb Center is made easier by the fact that the general public is always interested in plants and flowers.

The creativity and ingenuity of these promotional efforts is almost endless. Editors, garden clubs, and schools are provided with material that can be used as the basis for articles and other published pieces.

Triumph Tulips

Bloom in April
Height: 18 to 20 inches
This class of tulips was developed from a crossing between Single Early tulips and Darwins. They are exceptionally hardy flowers and are well suited for the garden or as breeders.

1. Aureola
2. Lustige Witwe
3. Don Quixote
4. Prominence
5. Hibernia
6. Kees Nelis
7. Garden Party

Foreign cities receive complimentary shipments of bulbs for their parks and other public areas (see pages 25, 66, 78, 79); Dutch bulb flowers are entered in international exhibitions; horticulturists participate in international conferences and meetings. Even the work carried out at the plant research station of Michigan State University under the direction of Professor M. den Hertogh (a good Dutch name!) receives financial support from the Dutch.

Because of the special nature of the bulb and its growing cycle, some activities have to be planned well in advance. Such was the case with Dutch participation in America's celebration of her Bicentennial in 1976 (see page 78). The Bulb Center was involved in the sessions of various committees set up in the United States as early as 1974 to plan the 1976 celebration. In the summer of 1975, a shipment of one million bulbs arrived in the United States from Holland. They were distributed with much fanfare among a number of municipalities, complete with a "Miss Tulip" who actually was the daughter of a bulb grower. Because of her background, she was invited to give talks and lectures, appeared on radio and television, and was interviewed by the editors of gardening magazines. The publicity for Dutch bulbs that resulted was far more than had been expected, thereby proving the appeal of bulb flowers in America. When the bulbs bloomed in the spring of 1976—almost as a herald of the momentous anniversary that would be celebrated in July of that year—a second wave of interest in Dutch bulbs developed. This, and much more, has contributed to Holland's image as the land of tulips.

4 Tulips In and Around the World

The hundreds of thousands of foreign tourists drawn each year to the bulb region of Holland are in for a pleasant surprise they may not have expected. None of the folders or guide books mentions it, and the Dutch National Tourist Board would not encourage it. But it soon becomes apparent to the tourist that the Dutch love of flowers is as dramatically expressed in their living rooms as in their well-tended bulb fields. Their passion for decorating the front window sills in such a way as to invite the gazes of passersby is evident in every village and town in the bulb district (see pages 110, 111).

Practically every Dutch household is filled with a profusion of flowers and plants. The front yards are no less well tended, for great care goes into transforming the small plots of land, often no larger than a small American driveway, into a horticultural paradise. A walk through the streets and lanes of the villages is a unique experience— one that the tourist will not soon forget.

As fall approaches, these visitors to Holland's bulb fields and flower-bedecked villages begin to think of planting tulips in their

own gardens; thus, they begin to look more closely at colors and shap[...]
and also to ask questions.

What to Buy

When planning a tulip bed, the first question always is: "Which tulips
should I plant?" You will find it best to inquire at a reliable nursery or
to consult the catalogues supplied by the better-known seed and bulb
companies. Most of these handle Dutch bulbs, and through these
dealers the home gardener is able to buy tulip bulbs of superior
quality. Lists at the back of the book will provide ideas for the varieties
to use for your purposes and some colors and companion plantings to
try in your own garden.

But be warned: The tulips you see at a flower show may not be sold
commercially. Oftentimes, only a very limited number of bulbs are
available of a new variety, and these are usually reserved for the
hybridizer or grower.

It is possible to tell at first sight whether a bulb is healthy. Bare
bulbs—bulbs without their outer covering—damage easily and are
more susceptible to disease. It does not matter if the brown skin of the
bulb is torn: these small blemishes, called "growing tear," are the fault
of Mother Nature, not the grower or the merchant. Growing tears
occur as a result of sharp changes in soil temperature during growth
and do not affect the quality of the bulb. "Handle bulbs as you would

Darwin Tulips

Bloom in May
Height: 24 to 26 inches
These tulips were developed by E. H. Krelage in 1889 from breeder tulips that he obtained in Belgium. They reached the height of their popularity in the 20s. They are characterized by brilliant colors and, because of their sturdiness, are ideal for the garden.

1. Sweet Harmony
2. Queen of Night
3. American Flag
4. Sunkist

eggs" is an old saying in the trade, one that is often posted in bulb sheds and sorting rooms throughout the Dutch bulb region.

The size of the bulb is directly related to the result that can be expected. Freshly harvested bulbs show the great variation in size that exists among the bulbs of the same variety grown in the same field. It is not the diameter but the circumference of the bulb that is measured; thus, a bulb classed as size 10 has a circumference of 10 centimeters (about 4 inches).

Bulbs are sorted by machines that are a far cry from the manual sorting of years ago. A conveyor belt drops the bulbs onto a vibrating, rubber-covered surface with holes of various sizes in it. The rubber covering protects the bulbs from damage. The openings are small at one end and gradually become larger towards the other. The smallest bulbs fall through the smallest holes, the larger bulbs into larger holes, and so on. Despite mechanization, the bulbs are spot-checked by hand for size, once they have dropped into the baskets. The checkers use a small, hand-held board with holes corresponding to the standard bulb sizes (see page 77). If a bulb falls through the size 12 hole but lands in the size 11 basket, it is classed as a size 11 bulb. Size 11 is large enough to assure good results, incidentally, but smaller sizes are not recommended. An exception to this rule is the Botanical tulip, which has a bulb often no larger than size 3 or 4—that is, 3 or 4 centimeters (about 1½ inches) in circumference. It still produces a beautiful flower. Bulbs for cultivation indoors should be size 12.

5. Landseadel's Supreme
6. Magi.
7. Pink Attraction
8. Clara Butt
9. Aristocrat
10. Cantor
11. Duke of Wellington

Colors and Classes

There is almost no limit to the colors and shades known to man, and tulips are found in more than half of them. Today's tulips come in a range of color from white to the darkest purple, in the softest tints of pink and rose to a brilliant red, from pale yellow to the color of fire, in stripes and streaks, in silver or even ivory tones, and with fringed and shaded edges.

As for the shapes of the blossoms, they are as varied as the colors—oval-shaped, star-shaped, with pointed petals, or with square bases. The stems are sometimes 36 inches tall, sometimes so short that the blossoms seem to rest on the earth.

By choosing carefully, you can have tulips blooming in your garden from early March through late May and into the warmer weeks of early summer.

These are the major classifications of tulips. Greater detail on these has been given in Chapter 1.

Early Tulips

Single Early Tulips (see page 82)   Outstanding is the six-petaled 'Brilliant Star,' 9 to 16 inches tall and pleasantly scented.

Double Early Tulips (see pages 84, 85)   Like 'Peach Blossom,' many-petaled, long-lasting flowers on stout stems 9 to 16 inches tall.

Mid-Season Tulips

Mendel Tulips (see page 87)   These are principally the result of a cross between the old Duc van Tol and Darwin tulips.

Triumph Tulips (see pages 88–89)   These resulted from a cross between Single Early tulips and Late (May-flowering) tulips. They have a larger flower and are sturdier than the Mendel tulips.

Darwin Hybrid Tulips (see pages 94, 95)   The result of a cross between Darwin tulips and *Tulipa fosteriana,* and also those resulting from a cross between other kinds of tulips and the Botanical tulips that no longer show evidence of having been developed from the wild.

Late Tulips

Darwin Tulips (see page 91)   Large, deep-cupped, square-based blossoms, with long, very sturdy stems.

Lily-Flowered Tulips (see pages 96, 97)   Flowers whose petals are pointed and curled back.

Cottage or Single Late Tulips (see page 98)   The oval-shaped blossoms are quite different from the Darwins and the Lily-flowered tulips.

Darwin Hybrid Tulips

Bloom in April/May
Height: 24 inches
The first Darwin Hybrids were develped by
D. W. Lefeber in 1936 from a crossing
between *Tulipa fosteriana* Madame Lefeber
and a Darwin tulip. They are characterized
by large flowers on long stems.

1. Gudoshnik
2. Elizabeth Arden
3. Spring Song
4. Diplomat
5. Beauty of Apeldoorn
6. Golden Apeldoorn
7. Apeldoorn
8. Various Darwin hybrids.

Rembrandt Tulips   These are the so-called "broken" tulips. The blossoms are streaked or striped with various colors—brown, black, mahogany-black, apricot, red, pink, or purple on a base color of red, white, or yellow.

Parrot Tulips (see pages 101, 102)   Sometimes called Parakeet tulips, these late-blooming tulips have fringed edges.

Double Late Tulips   This variety is also known as *Peony-flowered tulips*.

Species Tulips (The tulips and their varieties and hybrids that are recognizably wild)

Kaufmanniana (see page 105)   Very early, and very often with patterned leaves.

Fosteriana (see page 104)   The large, early tulips that sometimes have striped or spotted leaves.

Greigii (see pages 102, 103)   These bloom later than Kaufmanniana and have striped or spotted leaves.

Many Other Species   Also, their own varieties and hybrids.

Where to Plant

Tulips can be planted in many different situations, in full sun or in light shade. For the mixed border, plant the Single Early tulips—more hardy than the Darwins and Cottage tulips. These Single Earlies range in height from about 10 inches to 16 inches. They can withstand the strong winds of March, and they produce great splashes of color in the garden when everyone is looking for the brightness of spring.

The Double Early tulips, too, are fine for the mixed border, actually lasting much longer—both in the garden and as cut flowers—than the Early Single tulips. Both kinds, incidentally, are equally fine for forcing indoors. Parrot tulips, which are later-blooming, contribute to the beauty of a mixed border, as they continue the display into late spring.

Shrubs and hedges make striking backgrounds for tulips (see page 111), and since many of them bloom at about the same time as the spring flowering shrubs, by combining the two, and planting the tulips in drifts in the foreground, dramatic displays can be created. These are the Mid-Season tulips, those that also combine well with other flowering bulbs such as hyacinths, daffodils, crocuses, and muscari—the lovely blue grape-hyacinths that are so useful as an edging around the taller bulbs.

Rock gardens are ideal show cases for the so-called Botanical or Species tulips and their hybrids. These bloom ahead of all others. In

Lily-Flowered Tulips

Bloom in May
Height: 20 to 22 inches
These flowers were developed from a class
of Single Late-blooming tulips (origin:
Tulipa retroflexa) and subsequently became
an independent class as a result of an
increase in the number of varieties. Lily-
flowered tulips should be planted in a
sheltered spot in the garden. Because of the
sculpted shape of their petals, they are
attractive as cut flowers.

1. China Pink
2. Maytime
3. Marietta

fact, they often bloom before the last traces of snow have vanished,
and, depending upon the varieties planted, can continue to bloom
until the last of May. They are the short-stemmed, hardy plants that
are characterized by the beautifully patterned leaves that create a
stunning contrast with their blossoms. Some of the small bulbs, such as
chionodoxa, muscari, and crocuses, can be used with them in the rock
garden.

The Species tulips, hardier than the others, can be left safely in the
ground from year to year. They will continue to bloom for many years,
making it unnecessary to dig them up at the end of the season, a
difficult task in the crevices and pockets of a rock garden.

Tulipa eichleri and *Tulipa sylvestris*, both Species tulips, are also
well suited for planting in a woodland garden. Clump the bulbs
together for best effect. The shade and filtered sun will give the bulbs
plenty of light, and after they have been planted they will need no
further attention. The natural mulch provided by the trees will keep
the bulbs weed-free and will maintain the soil in good condition, with
plenty of humus.

Proper Soil for Tulips

Bulbs need a very well-drained soil. When preparing the tulip bed, dig
it down to 16 or 18 inches (see page 113), add humus and peat moss. If
the soil has a tendency toward clay, also add sand or perlite. In the

bottom of the hole where the tulip is to be planted, drop a handful of sand or perlite so as to insure good drainage—otherwise, the bulb may rot. Fertilizer and bone meal should be added when the soil is being prepared.

Planting Depth

Bulbs should be planted at least 5 or 6 inches deep, depending on the kind and size of bulb. However, those that are planted much deeper— to 12 inches—will continue to bloom for several more years than those planted at a more shallow depth. Not so many small bulbs are formed if the parent bulb has been planted, say, 10 to 12 inches down, and this makes for fewer but sturdier new bulbs, which produce better blossoms.

There is another reason for deep planting. Mice and other rodents are particularly fond of tulip bulbs, and if you find that your tulips are not coming up as you had thought they should, the answer may be that the animals have eaten them. The deeper the planting, the less available the bulbs to the chipmunks, moles, and mice. You can also protect your bulbs from rodents by planting them in wire cages. Also, deep-planted bulbs, being better protected, are less subject to attack by botrytis blight.

One more good reason for deep planting: It makes it possible to put in other spring- and summer-flowering plants over the tulips, so that

Bloom in May
Height: 20 to 22 inches
These tulips are also known as "Cottage Tulips" due to their origin in the gardens of English cottages. As a result of many crossings, the flowers have come to lose the variations in shape which once characterized them.

1. Aristocrat
2. Princess Margaret Rose
3. Rosy Wings
4. Mrs. John T. Scheepers
5. Halcro
6. Burgundy Lace
7. Greenland

when the bulbs have finished blooming the garden can continue to be colorful. The tulip foliage must be allowed to die without being cut off. This gives the bulb food for the next season's bloom. If annuals or other plants are set out amongst the tulips, they will hide the browning foliage and keep the garden beautiful. The dead tulip blossoms should be cut off to prevent the forming of seed, which would deplete the energy in the bulb.

The danger of deep planting is that the bulbs will rot if the soil is poorly drained. But if the flower bed has been properly prepared, to a depth of at least 16 inches, and if plenty of sand, humus, and peat moss has been added, the advantages are great.

Depth of planting is always measured from the top of the planted bulb to the surface of the soil. So that to plant a bulb 5 inches deep, you must dig a hole 7 or more inches deep, depending on the size of the bulb.

There are, however, reasons for planting the bulbs at the more conventional depth of 5 to 6 inches. If you are experimenting with color and plant combinations, for instance, you may not be satisfied with your first try. In that case, dig them up after their foliage has died down and replant them in a spot more likely to produce the effect you are after. The shallower the bulbs are planted, the easier it will be to find them.

It is best not to plant tulips in the same bed year after year. Most of the nourishment of the soil will have been used up by the old bulbs,

and if by chance the old bulbs have been attacked by botrytis
(a problem that will be taken up and discussed later in this chapter),
the disease will still be in the soil and will be transmitted to any bulbs
in the same place.

In replanting an old bed, you must prepare the soil to a depth of 15
to 18 inches and add fertilizer and humus.

How to Plant

With a trowel, dig a hole for each bulb to the depth you have chosen.
Place a small handful of sand in the bottom of the hole, place the bulb,
flat side down, on the sand, and fill up the hole with soil. Press firmly
to make sure no air pockets remain.

It is possible to use the dibble method, if the soil is sufficiently
light. Make a small hole to the proper depth with a pointed stick, drop
the bulb in, and firmly press soil round the bulb.

Or, of course, if you are preparing a large bed and remove the soil
in the process, it is easier to place the bulbs in the desired arrangement
and at the proper depth before returning the topsoil to the bed.

Large tulips should be planted about 8 inches apart so that the
plants will have plenty of room for root growth and so they will flourish
and bloom well. The small, so-called "botanical bulbs," should be
planted in clusters closer together, the better to create an effect of
masses of color.

Parrot Tulips

Bloom in May
Height: 20 to 22 inches
Popular tulips for use as a border

1. Texas Gold
2. Karel Doorman
3. Flaming Parrot

1

Planting Tulips Outside

1. Buy bulbs from a reputable dealer.
2. Make a hole for each bulb or
3. Dig a small, shallow pit for a number of tulip bulbs.
4. Put the bulbs in the ground firmly, with the narrow end pointing up.
5. Cover the bulbs with soil.
6. Water the bulbs thoroughly. If the ground is extremely dry, wait until the water has had a chance to seep in and repeat the watering process.
7. The tulips will begin to form roots during the winter months.

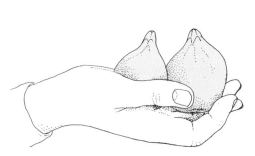

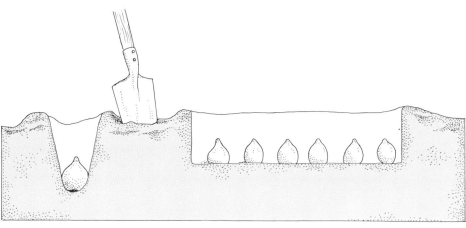

4. Orange Favourite
5. Blue Parrot
6. Black Parrot

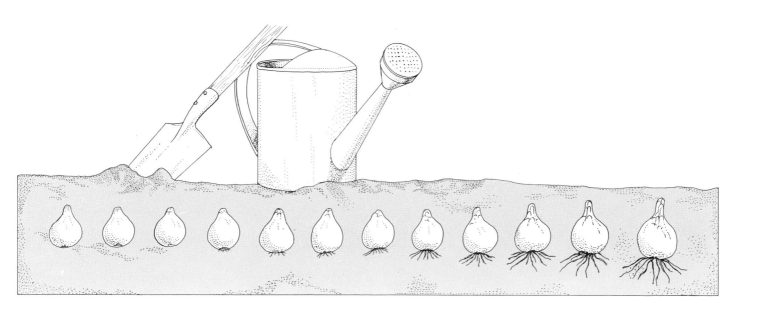

Greigii Hybrids

Bloom in April
Height: 8 to 16 inches
Purple-ish strips and spots on ribbed leaves
are notable characteristics of these flowers.
There is considerable difference in height
from one variety to another. Large flowers
with striking color combinations make them
ideal additions to any garden, especially
rock gardens.

1. Red Riding Hood
2. Cape Cod

Once the bulbs are planted, place a label near each clump. A tongue depressor works well for this. Print the name of the variety on it with indelible ink. It takes six months for the tulips to bloom, and even the most astute gardeners often forget which variety is planted exactly where. A good alternative arrangement is to draw a sketch of your garden, and then list the names of the varieties you have chosen for each section of the plan.

When to Plant

October and November are the best tulip-planting times. There is actually only one rule to follow: plant before the first frost. The roots of the bulbs must be sufficiently developed before the frost comes to withstand the winter and survive to bloom in the spring.

If you live in an area that encounters heavy frost, after the ground has frozen put a layer of peat moss over the tulip beds to help protect them. The peat need not be removed in spring. It will improve the quality of the soil.

In warm areas, such as the southern states of the United States, a different situation prevails. There tulip bulbs must be stored at a temperature of about 40° F. for a period of eight weeks before planting. But they can be planted in the middle of January and will bloom in about eight to ten weeks.

3. Pandour
4. Plaisir
5. Oriental Beauty

Fertilizing

Tulips will do best if they are given a well-balanced diet. Early in spring, apply a combination of wood ashes, superphosphate, and 5–10–5 (5% nitrogen, 10% phosphoric acid, 5% potash). Most gardeners still favor the addition of bone meal in preparing the beds. A fertilizer high in nitrogen should be avoided as it will produce growth dangerously early.

Mulching

A mulching of peat moss or wood ashes will keep your tulips weed-free. Put on the mulch as soon as the leaves begin to show in spring. If it is applied too early—that is, before growth appears above ground—the mulch will tend to hold early spring rains and keep the ground soggy. As a result, the tulip bulbs might rot.

If weeds should appear despite the mulch, pull them by hand. Be sure not to try to use a hoe, for this sharp tool could easily damage the bulbs.

Diseases

No matter how successful they may be, no matter how influential they may have been in promoting the tulip's popularity, all tulip growers

Fosteriana Hybrids

Bloom in April
Height: 14 to 24 inches
Characterized by large, clearly colored
flowers on strong stems. Ideal for
planting with exotic, short-stemmed
bulb flowers such as Muscari (Blue
Grape Hyacinth) and Chionodoxa.

opposite above:
1. Orange Emperor
2. Candela
3. Madame Lefeber

Kaufmanniana Hybrids

Bloom in March
Height: 6 to 8 inches
T. kaufmanniana originated in Turkestan
and are also known as the "waterlily
tulips." They have short stems and
magnificent colors, and, in early spring,
lend splashes of color to any garden.

right:
1. Shakespeare
2. Stresa
3. Heart's Delight

opposite below: Holland's Keukenhof
Park in tulip time.

face one common enemy: plant disease. In Holland great efforts are being made to combat this threat.

Obviously, healthy bulbs are essential for the production of the high-quality flowers for which Dutch bulbs have come to be known. In order to maintain this reputation, the Dutch growers have established their own Plant Disease Inspection Service, which operates
under Dutch Government supervision. If a particular lot of tulip bulbs meets the service's high standards, it is issued a certificate of quality. The Dutch government also periodically inspects bulb crops, both in the field and at bulb auctions. The Bulb Research Laboratory in Lisse continues to work on discovering the cause of and cure for diseases that threaten the bulb industry. This, combined with the laboratory's work on creating new varieties, will assure the future of the Dutch bulb industry.

This means, of course, that your bulbs are likely to be healthy when you buy them. However, there is one disease that might attack your tulips. This is the well-known Tulip Fire, or botrytis. It spreads so fast, once started, that it earned the title of Fire.

The first symptoms of botrytis are a yellowing and shriveling of the tips of the leaves, and spots along the edges of the leaves. As the flowers open, dark spots appear on light-colored petals and light spots on dark petals. This is followed by a mold that spreads on leaves and flowers.

The tulips pictured on these pages belong to
the Botanical class. They are species of wild
tulips, and can withstand rugged weather
conditions.

1. Johann Strauss (Kaufmannia hybrid),
   blooms in March
   (8 inches high)
2. *Tulipa tarda*,
   blooms in April
   (4 inches high)
3. *Tulipa turkestanica*,
   blooms in March
   (8 inches high)
4. *Tulipa kolpakowskiana*,
   blooms in April
   (6 inches high)
5. *Tulipa marjoletti*,
   blooms in May
   (20 inches high)
6. *Tulipa praestans* 'Fusilier',
   blooms in March
   (10 inches high)

1   2

Botrytis attacks tulips most often if the season is warm and wet while the plants are developing. It can be controlled to some extent by the removal of affected leaves and petals. But as soon as such symptoms appear, the plants should be sprayed thoroughly with ferbam, or zineb, or with a Bordeaux mixture. If this doesn't work, pull up the plants and discard them.

If botrytis appears in your garden, take care the following year to plant tulips in another spot where tulips have not grown for several years, and put them in full sun. Before planting the bulbs, examine them carefully and throw away any that have little dark specks either on the brown outside skins or on the base of the bulb. These specks carry the botrytis disease.

Lifting your Bulbs

Tulip bulbs can, of course, be left in the ground from year to year, but the blossoms will get smaller and smaller and eventually the bulbs will completely die out. Digging them up and replanting the largest of the new bulbs is the rather tedious alternative. The easiest way to do it, however, is to plant the bulbs in plastic flower pots and sink them in the ground about 4 to 5 inches under the surface (see page 112). At normal planting time, take up the pots, and shake out the bulbs. All that will remain of the original bulb will be some loose layers of the old outer covering, and these should be discarded. A number of new,

Planting Tulips in a Flower Box or Tray

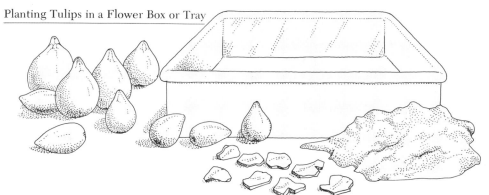

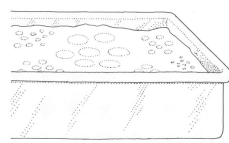

1. Tulips are well suited for planting in a flower box or in a tray outdoors.

2. Use soil that has been mixed with a fair amount of peat moss so that the soil will retain sufficient water.

3. When buying bulbs for planting in this manner, be sure to take their color and size into account.

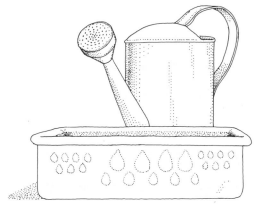

4. By placing bulbs near each other and by planting them at different depths you will create an attractive arrangement.

5. After planting the bulbs, cover them with a layer of soil and water them. The ground must remain moist.

6. By adding other plants (for example, aubrietia or even small evergreens) you will have a pleasing mini-garden.

smaller bulbs will remain in its place. The larger ones should be replanted. These will flourish and bloom for several more years, until the time comes when they, too, begin to dwindle and must be dug up and replaced.

The smallest of the new bulbs will not be ready for planting. These can be kept in a box of moist soil at a temperature of about 60°F. for two years—either in a basement or a garage, or wherever the temperature remains fairly constant—when they too will be ready to plant. These small new ones can also be planted in a corner of the garden where they can be left for two years while they grow and develop into bulbs large enough to produce fine blossoms at full scale and full color.

The Botanical tulips, the so-called Species tulips, when left in the ground, will continue to bloom much longer than most other kinds. However, their life, too, can be further prolonged by using this same method.

Tulips in Containers

With the increased popularity of high-rise apartments and condominiums, balconies and roof gardens play an important role in the life of the occupant—it is his principal contact with nature, with the world outside the window. Decorating balconies with plants is growing ever more popular, as you will notice in any large urban area. But

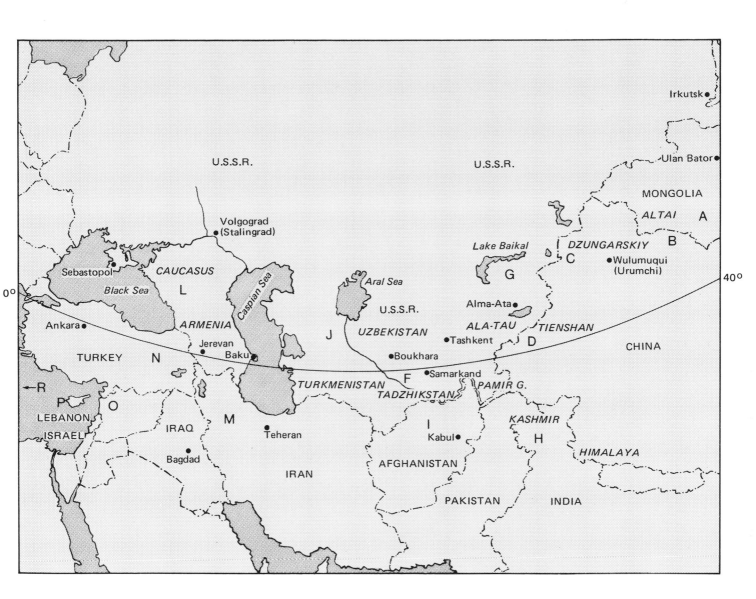

The Birthplace of the Tulips

The Species tulips, which have been used in the development of many new tulip varieties (e.g., *T. kaufmanniana*, *greigii*, *fosteriana*, *praestans*, *eichleri*), originate in a "corridor" which stretches along the 40° latitude between Northern China and Southern Europe. Although not shown on the map, several varieties have been found also in the Kiangsi, Tsekiang, Hupeh, and Shantung provinces of China and in Korea, Manchuria, and Japan; and some varieties are even native to Northern Italy, Switzerland, Southern France, the Iberian peninsula, and in the Atlas mountain range of North Africa.

There are few flowers as versatile as the tulip. By carefully selecting the right color and size, the gardener can plant the tulip anywhere: in the garden, in a container, or in a flower box. Those who do not have a garden can plant them indoors.

containers should not be restricted to balconies and roof gardens—patios, doorsteps, and decks are all suited to container gardening. Handsome pots, wooden tubs, half-barrels, strawberry jars, and ceramic containers are all useful for growing bulbs (see above and pages 111–112).

The Botanical tulips, with their shorter stems, are ideally suited to this type of gardening, and other bulb flowers will continue the season long after the tulips have stopped blooming.

Long, rectangular flower boxes are the best containers for balconies. Whatever sort of container you use, punch holes in the bottom to permit good drainage. Place a layer of newspapers in the bottom—this will prevent the soil from leaking out. Fill the container with soil and plant the bulbs 5 or 6 inches below the surface, leaving at least 2 or 3 inches of soil below the bulbs to give the roots sufficient room to grow. Store the containers for three months in a garage or basement area where there is no danger of freezing. The ideal temperature is 40° F. or 9° C. In early spring put the planters in place, and as the spring sunshine begins to warm the soil your bulbs will begin to bloom.

Forcing for Indoor Bloom

Not everyone is fortunate enough to have his own yard, but everyone can enjoy the beauty of flowers indoors. Potted tulips have a place in

Even if you do enjoy the luxury of a garden,
you can still plant tulips indoors to grace a
windowsill and bridge the gap between
indoors and outdoors.

your living room, just as cut flowers do, and tulips grown indoors can
be enjoyed long before those outdoors are ready to bloom. A list of
bulbs suitable for forcing is given on page 128.

Plant the pots in the fall. A quart of soil will roughly fill a 5-inch pot
(see page 112). If potting soil is not readily available, use a mixture of
equal parts of sand, ordinary garden soil, and peat moss. Place a few
shards in the bottom of the pot to be sure of good drainage. (If the pot
does not have a drainage hole, take care not to overwater.)

The soil should be as deep below the bulbs as the bulbs are high, so
that the roots will have enough room to grow. Place the bulbs firmly in
the soil with the nose of the bulb just barely showing. For a beautiful
display of color, plant several bulbs in one pot. A 6-inch pot can hold 6
to 8 bulbs, but don't let the bulbs touch each other.

Water the pot thoroughly, and set it in the refrigerator at a
temperature of about 40°F. (8° or 9° centigrade). Leave the pot in the
refrigerator for 10–16 weeks, watering lightly once a week. Then place
the pot in a sunny window—and wait for the tulips' spring display.

Some Tips on Conditioning
and Arranging Tulips

It doesn't matter how few or how many tulips you have for your
bouquet—one bright red tulip in the proper setting can be quite

Growing Tulips Indoors

Use a pot with a drainage hole in the bottom. Mix equal portions of sand, soil, and peat moss. Cover the bottom of the pot with a shard or some gravel. Fill the pot half full with the soil mixture and water it thoroughly. Put in the bulbs—but not too close together. Cover them with the soil mixture and water again. Cover the pots, and set them in a cool spot for 12 to 16 weeks. (They can also be buried outdoors, but they should then be covered with 3 to 4 inches of earth and protected by a covering of straw; the straw should then be watered thoroughly.

dramatic and three or more will give a feeling of affluence. Because of the long stems, tulips are apt to arrange themselves and can present the most charming appearance when left to form a natural grouping. The first responsibility of the flower arranger is to prepare the flowers properly and then keep them in a fairly cool spot. If fresh, they will last five to eight days.

Cutting or Buying Your Flowers

Choose flowers that are the size of fat buds. They should not be too tight or they may not open, but of course you do not want them so far along that they open up and fall in one day. Be sure they are not limp. Water will not revive flowers already dying. Cut as few leaves as possible—they should be left to provide food for the bulbs. Foilage from other plants will set them off beautifully.

Conditioning

The best way to prepare the tulips is to cut an inch or so off the stem, wrap them in a cone of wet newspaper (or wax paper), about a dozen at a time, and stand in a bucket full of cold water. The water should be deep enough to reach almost to the blossom, and if you use newspaper, it should be under water, too, so that it will not dry out. Let them stand overnight.

Arranging

It is best to choose a vase that measures about ⅔ the depth of the tulips' stems so that they will have plenty of water. This depth will also give you more control of the placement of the flowers. Cut the stems to different lengths, and you will have a more graceful and natural looking arrangement; each tulip will appear to better advantage and the bouquet will have shape (see below). Keep the arrangement out of the heat and sun and be sure to add cool, fresh water every day. If you are arranging flowers for a show, you might want to use an extra trick to keep them up to par for the duration. For instance, if you drop some cooled, melted candle wax of the same color as the flower into the bottom of the cup the petals will not fall. And if you must make a particular line with the stem, use florists' wire, running it up through the stem to the blossom. In that way you can hold it in just the position most desirable for your design.

If you would like to copy some of the flower paintings of the early Dutch masters, you will find that, while using no more than three tulips in an arrangement, the painters invariably chose flowers available at different times of the year. Substitute seasonal blossoms of the same general appearance as the originals to produce the best results.

Always keep your containers scrubbed and clean so that there will be no bacteria left to foul the water. Try different shapes, sizes, and colors of containers for your tulips. You may find the perfect vase unexpectedly. And always keep the arrangement in clear sight so that you may get as much enjoyment as possible while they last.

Appendices

Tulips
in America

Tulips and Roses by George Harvey
(c. 1800/01-1878). This oil on academy
board was painted by the artist in 1847.
Born in England, Harvey came to the
United States when he was twenty and
lived in the West, in Brooklyn, and in
Boston before building his own home near
Hastings-on-Hudson in 1833. He helped
design Washington Irving's "Sunnyside"
and painted a notable series of American
scenes in watercolor while living in that
area.

"In no class of plants has nature so varied her delicate tints as in this,"
wrote William Prince in the 1828 edition of *A Short Treatise on
Horticulture.* "It would seem as if each change which nature or art is
capable of forming, was included in the varying beauties of the Tulip,
above 1100 varieties of which are cultivated in some of the gardens of
Holland. All the finer varieties, however, of this delightful flower have
been obtained by cultivation and art during the last two centuries,
through the perseverance of the Dutch, French, and Flemish florists;
several kinds of which possess a delightful fragrance, although persons
who are ignorant of this circumstance have made the want of it an
objection to this splendid flower."

This high opinion of the tulip, recorded by Mr. Prince, was widely
held long before his time and has been held constantly to the present.
It is quite evident that some early settlers in the colonies brought tulip
bulbs with them as part of their household gear and others made
arrangements for them to be sent over from Europe, along with various
seeds and plants. Adrian van der Donck, visiting in the New World in
1655, wrote back of the vegetables and ornamentals his fellow
countrymen had succeeded in raising in New Amsterdam and named
the tulip as one of them. They say the famous governor, Peter
Stuyvesant, grew tulips in his gardens, and we know that tulips must
have been grown on the estate of Van Cortlandt Manor, the Dutch
colonial house at Croton-on-Hudson, N.Y. It was built in 1681, and
about 1732 a portrait was painted showing a child standing beside a
vase of mixed flowers—one of which was the tulip.

Mrs. Wynant Van Zandt. Painted in oil on canvas by an unidentified artist, Mrs. Van Zandt (1692–1772) was born Catharina Ten Eyck and became Wynant's second wife in 1710. This portrait of her, holding the tulip in her hand, was painted around 1725.

The German colonists in Pennsylvania (called the "Pennsylvania-Dutch") were gifted and prolific craftsmen, and the tulip seems to have been one of their most popular decorative motifs. It was used on quilts, cast-iron stoves, headstones, butter molds, boxes, and pottery. Shown here is a box for treasures, almost completely covered with tulips. (See also page 121.)

It was not just the early Dutch settlers in New Amsterdam who planted tulips but also the colonists in New England and the Atlantic states. In a Boston newspaper dated March 30, 1760, appeared a list of seeds available from a local nursery, and it included "50 Different Sorts of Mixed Tulip Roots." And in Boston, also, Thomas Hancock (the uncle of the statesman John Hancock) had a typical but exasperating experience with ordering plants by mail. He was dealing with an English firm in an attempt to get some fruit trees he desired, and on December 20, 1736, he wrote thanking the dealer for trees and seeds received. "I return you my hearty thanks for the Plumb Tree and Tulip Roots you were pleased to make me a Present off, which are very acceptable to me. . . ." However, on June 24, 1737, he wrote that none of his seeds had come up: "The garden seeds and Flower seeds which you sold Mr. Wilks for me and Charged me £16 4s. 2d. Sterling were not worth one farthing . . . ," with a P.S.: "The Tulip Roots you were pleased to make a present off to me are all Dead as well."

Meanwhile, in Pennsylvania in 1698, John Tateham's "Great and Stately Palace . . . which is pleasantly situated out the North side of Town" had tulips in its garden, according to a report made to William Penn by one Gabriel Thomas.

Jefferson, in his *Garden Book*, mentions his tulips in planting lists and daily progress records. He was so fond of his garden that when he was away from home (as he was so often while serving his country in Philadelphia and Washington), he expected one of his family to keep him informed as to how the plants were growing, what was in bloom,

117

German colonists brought with them the custom of recording their birth, baptismal, and wedding certificates on handmade paper decorated with homemade inks. The style of writing used on these documents was called *fractur* after a 16th-century German type face. And not only did the first paper-makers use a tulip as the watermark in the paper, but the teacher or clergyman who wrote and decorated the *Taufschein*(birth and baptism records) often drew tulip shapes around the text. When used on these records, a three-petaled tulip represented the Trinity. The handmade paper was so sturdy that many of these fracturs have survived the years and can be found on display in museums and private collections. Shown here is a birth and baptismal record by the Cross-legged Angel Artist (c. 1805). Bibles, songbooks, bookplates, and house blessings (*Haus-segen*) were often embellished in the same way.

and when each bud first appeared. On April 14, 1808, his granddaughter Ellen W. Randolph wrote him: "I won't say anything of the flower beds that is sister Anns part. . . . The sheep eat up 4 orange trees and bit half of the finest off besides. . . They are all mean little things except that which the sheep bit, but they are very young." And sister Anne wrote: "I have been twice to Monticello to see the sesamum & Governor Lewis's pea planted. The hyacinths were in bloom, they are superb ones. the Tulips are all buding. neither the hyacinths nor Tulips grow as regularly this spring as they did the last. Wormley in taking them up left some small roots in the ground which have come up about in the bed & not in the rows with the others. . . ."

Both in Colonial Williamsburg and the garden at George Mason's home—Gunstan Hall (1755)—the gardens are kept planted with flowers, such as tulips, known to have been in the original beds. When North Carolina's first state capital, Tryon Palace at New Bern, was restored in 1952–59, and the gardens laid out, tulips were included. Although there were no definite records at the time, tulips are known to have been typical of the time and place.

During the 1800s, Frederick Law Olmstead, the best known of our landscape architects, was planning many large and famous gardens—both public and private. Central Park in New York and the City of Boston Park system were examples of his control of space and the successful use he made of it. Biltmore Gardens in Asheville, North Carolina, was one private garden he planned to please George Washington Vanderbilt, owner of Biltmore House. Olmstead designed

Like the architecture of The
Frick Collection in New York
City, the garden there is a tasteful re-
creation of aristocratic, 18th-century
France. In the spring tulips bloom
with all the order and symmetry, the
refinement and elegance typical of
the period evoked.

vast formal gardens, shaped within by hedges; they were a natural
setting for tulips, and indeed tulips were the featured flower every
spring. In 1858 at "Old White" Garden, The Greenbrier, masses of
tulips were planted, too. Both of these gardens are kept as they were
with the old flowers and may be visited today.

The first chartered college in the state of New York was Union
College in Schenectady. It also lays claim to being the first to have
planned its grounds. These were not laid out until 1813, although the
college was founded in 1795. About 1833, Professor Isaac W. Jackson
planned and planted what became known as Jackson's Garden. Over
the years, his missionary students sent him many plants for the garden,
and included in these were some early Botanical tulips from China.
Two more recent events have brought Union College a different kind
of importance. Scenes from the movie *The Way We Were*, starring
Barbra Streisand, were played there, and it is, moreover, the place
where Jimmy Carter studied nuclear physics.

It was also in the early 1800s that many of the Dutch, who were
crossing the ocean in search of a new and better life, pushed on into the
Middle Western states to settle. They brought with them their tulip
bulbs, and many of the settlers found ideal growing conditions for this
plant. As we have seen in Chapter II, the tulip flourishes in the Middle
West, and several important festivals are held there annually.

For the Chicago Century of Progress Exposition in 1934, a large
tract of land was put aside in Michigan City, Indiana, for an
International Friendship Garden. Many countries assisted in setting

up the individual gardens, and Holland contributed 200,000 tulip
bulbs. More have been planted over the years, and "Tulips on Parade"
now opens the Garden every year in May.

Although during tulipomania, and indeed for many years
afterwards, the broken tulip was cherished in Holland, England, and
all of Europe where the tulip was grown, the solid-colored flowers are
now most in evidence in America. They are treasured for the blaze of
color possible when used in quantity; they also give the gardener the
feeling of an artist with brilliant paints to splash upon his canvas.

Even for people who have no gardens, tulips have become an
important part of life. Because they do make such a show, they are
invaluable in large open spaces such as public parks, and have been
used for the purpose extensively. In New York City, for example, the
Parks Department plants thousands of bulbs each year—at Battery
Park, Park Plaza, City Hall, Fort Tryon Park, the Museum of Natural
History, the New York Public Library, and in the Conservatory
Gardens in Central Park. New York City was fortunate enough to have
a concerned citizen, Mrs. Mary Lasker, who in 1955 underwrote the
experiment of planting tulips in the mall on Park Avenue. It was so
much admired that the hotels and office buildings lining the avenue
took over the responsibility of furnishing funds for the plantings in the
following years. The experiment has become a tradition, which
annually transforms median strips throughout the city into garden areas.

The many excellent sources for tulip bulbs available to all who live
in the United States make it unnecessary for individual American

gardeners to import bulbs—a tricky business because of the government restrictions. Some few dealers grow their own bulbs in this country, and others maintain bulb fields in Holland. In all likelihood, however, most of the bulbs you buy have been imported from a Dutch grower. They should all be good healthy bulbs if you order them from a reliable source and plant them as soon as possible after you get them. The following is a list of distributors, and when you write for a catalogue, ask for the fall edition.

Source List

Brown Bulb Ranch of Washington, Inc.
936 N.W. 49th Street
Seattle, Wa. 98107

Burnett Brothers, Inc.
92 Chambers Street
New York, N.Y. 10007

W. Atlee Burpee Company
Warminster, Pa. 18974
Clinton, Ia. 52732
Riverside, Cal. 92502
Sanford, Fla. 32771

P. de Jager & Sons Bulbs, Inc.
188 Asbury Street
South Hamilton, Mass. 01982

John Messelaar Bulb Co.
150 County Road
Route 1A
Ipswich, Ma. 01938

John Scheepers, Inc.,
63 Wall Street
New York, N.Y. 10005

Van Bourgondien Brothers
245 Farmingdale Road
P. O. Box A
Babylon, N.Y. 11702

Van Zonneveld's
810 Cassel Road
Collegeville, Pa. 19426

Tulips
in Great Britain

The illustrations on pages 122–124 were made during England's annual tulip festival at Spalding in the Lincolnshire Fens. After the tulips have been de-headed, in order to create stock for the dry bulb trade, the colorful petals are used to create magnificent and fanciful floats, which are then paraded along a four-mile route, to the delight of thousands of tulip-lovers.

Tulips have been grown in Great Britain since the 17th century when travellers would bring bulbs home to plant in their private gardens. In the middle of the eighteen hundreds a tulip society was formed but it was not until the end of the century that tulips started to be grown commercially. Bulbs were not available for the ordinary gardener, and when they first began to be marketed there were very few varieties available. The bulbs were grown in beds and lifted annually because the growers were, in these early days, supplying the cut-flower market in much larger quantities than the dry-bulb market. One of the early pioneers was a Mr. J. T. White, a scrap merchant by trade, who noticed tulips in the gardens of some of the houses he visited on his rounds and had the idea of starting a tulip farm. For the first quarter of the century, the industry was made up of small family concerns such as Culpina, Whites and Wellbrands. They were both wholesalers and retailers, and their first large orders were for supplying public parks.

Although tulips are grown all over Great Britain and Ireland and may be admired both in the herbaceous borders of cottage gardens and in the grander displays such as the beds in the royal parks, it is to the Lincolnshire Fens that we must go to find the home of the tulip in this country. In the sandy loam farmlands around Spalding, drained and reclaimed by Dutchmen for agricultural land three centuries earlier, more than half the acreage of bulbs in England are grown, making the landscape a blaze of color in springtime. In 1919, the Spalding and District Bulb Growing Association was formed and in the 1920s the

industry started to expand rapidly. Between the two world wars it flourished and the fame of the tulip fields grew, bringing greater crowds of sightseers every year.

During the Second World War there was a great reduction in the trade as gardens were turned over to the production of food. The tulip fields were also needed for the war effort, and the result was a shortage of supply which had the inevitable effect on prices. Between 1945 and 1946 the cut flowers were fetching as much as 17/5D (about $4.50) per dozen wholesale.

After the war the bulb industry again expanded, and for the furtherance of trade, plans were formed for a show garden where growers could display their goods and information be given to the public. A site was bought outside Spalding, and Carl Van Empelen, a famous landscape architect, designed the gardens. Work started in 1964, and in 1966 the garden, named Springfields, was opened to the public. Here people can walk through twenty-five acres of gardens and woodlands and glasshouses. Growers, wholesalers, and retailers each have their own plots in which to display their wares. There are literally hundreds of varieties of tulips growing on this one site, and they are at their best in the greenhouses. In April and in May the outdoor beds come to their full glory. Cut flowers are available on sale, and those wishing to purchase bulbs can see exactly what they are buying and at the same time receive any help or advice they might require. Some flower-lovers take a picnic and sit on benches in the glasshouses

surrounded by a rainbow of tulips, surely making the sandwiches taste better and aiding the digestion. The whole event becomes pleasurable and civilised.

Opposite the entrance to Springfields there is a statue of "Tulipan the Tulipman." This statue was unveiled in April 1972 by the Turkish ambassador to commemorate the 400th anniversary of the introduction of the tulip to Europe from Turkey in 1572.

The necessity to de-head tulips to improve stock for the dry bulb trade meant that the glorious tulip fields were no longer attractive when devoid of color, so in order to keep the interest of the sightseers, the Spalding Farmers Union conceived the idea of the tulip parade. Millions of tulip heads are used for the making of magnificent floats. A tulip queen competition is held prior to the event, and the winning girl becomes Miss Tulipland and rides on the leading float. The floats are modeled on a variety of subjects but most nowadays depict giant-size comic animals such as Dougal and the Magic Roundabout, a teddy bear, elephants, and Disney characters. The floats parade along a four-mile route and there is also a static display for those who want a closer look at the ingenuity and skillful work of the designs. This parade has become world-famous and attracts about 300,000 people to its show from every corner of the earth. So we may be grateful to the tulip, which, sacrificing her flower at the height of its beauty, yet, disembodied, still delights us in a most spectacular way, as can be seen in the pictures reproduced on pages 122–124.

Plant Combinations and Companions

Many enthusiastic home gardeners want to go beyond planting tulips in masses for sheer color, and they then become interested in special effects that can be made with the tulips in combination with other plants of contrasting heights, colors, and textures. Sometimes these plants may be used as a background for the tulips, sometimes to mask the dying foliage, and sometimes just to enhance their beauty. Gertrude Jekyll, the great 19th-century English gardener, suggests using *Stachys lanata* (Lamb's ears) as an underplanting, "The first small grey spires shooting up in spring, interlaced with milk-white tulips produce an almost ethereal effect." She also records a plan for a green garden whose flowers are nearly all white beginning with white tulips in the spring.

A garden plan that sounds delightful is described in a pamphlet about the gardens at the World's Fair of 1940 in New York. Designed by Mrs. Ray B. Levinson, it was a Blue and White Garden and silhouetted against an evergreen background planned to show continuing color by use of the proper plants throughout the season. In the spring, there was a screen of dogwoods and crabapples, several varieties of white tulips with different tints and heights, a border of forget-me-nots and plantings of blue phlox and pansies.

In her *Garden Book* V. Sackville-West tells of planting the Lady Tulip, *Tulipa clusiana*, amongst *Daphne retusa* and *collina*; she also tries using the creeping form of rosemary as a covering plant for the Lady Tulip.

In the Old Church Garden in Salem, Massachusetts, the focal point is an arbor covered with wisteria. Pink tulips were planted to complement the delicate lavender of its blossoms and together this makes a pastel plant combination of perfection.

A study of any good bulb catalogue will give you other ideas, as will further reading and visiting spring gardens. The few lists that follow should prove helpful as you begin to plan new uses for your tulips.

Some Good Companion Plants

(These all have blossoms whose colors harmonize with tulips.)
Arabis
Candytuft
English daisy
Forget-me-not
Lobelia
Pansies
Primroses
Violas
Wallflower

White Tulips

'Diana'—Single Early
'White Hawk'—Single Early
'Schoonoord'—Double Early
'Hibernia'—Triumph Tulip
'Kansas'—Triumph Tulip
'Athlete'—Mendel Tulip
'White Sail'—Mendel Tulip
'Magier' (flushed at edges with purple)
   —Darwin
'Glacier'—Darwin
'White Triumphator'—Lily-flowered
'Maureen'—Cottage
'Sorbet (flushed rose)—Cottage
'White Parrot'—Parrot
'Mount Tacoma'—Double Late
   (Peony-flowered)
'Ancilla'—Kaufmanniana

Pink Tulips

'Pink Beauty'—Single Early
'Christmas Marvel'—Single Early
'Peach Blossom'—Double Early
'Peerless Pink'—Triumph
'Dreaming Maid'—Triumph
'Garden Party'—Triumph
'Pink Trophy'—Mendel Tulip
'Clara Butt'—Darwin
'Aristocrat'—Darwin
'Rosy Wings'—Cottage
'Renown'—Cottage
'China Pink'—Lily-flowered
'Cordell Hull'—Rembrandt
'Fantasy'—Parrot Tulip
'Pink Supreme'—Double-Late
   (Peony-flowering)
'Pink Empress'—Fosteriana
'Pink Emperor'—Fosteriana

Fragrant Tulips*

Variety Name	Color	Type	Flowering Time
'Bellona'	Yellow	Early Single	April
'De Wet'	Orange	Early Single	April
'Doctor Plesman'	Orange-red	Early Single	April
'Prince of Austria'	Orange-Red	Early	April
'Peach Blossom'	Pink	Early Double	April
'Mrs. Van der Hoef'	Yellow	Early Double	April
Tulipa gesneriana	Crimson		May
Tulipa sylvestris	Yellow		May
Tulipa primulina	Yellow		May
Tulipa persica	Yellow		May–June
'Dido'	Cherry-Red	Cottage	May
'Ellen Willmott'	Primrose-Yellow	Lily-Flowered	May

*You may find many tulips that seem to be without scent will become fragrant when cut and brought indoors.

Some Tulips for Forcing

'Brilliant'	'Paul Richter'	'Hibernia'	'City of Haarlem'
'Star'	'Prominence'	'Peerless'	'Prince of Austria'
'Joffre'	'Bing Crosby'	'Golden Eddy'	'White Sail'
'Apricot Beauty'	'Bellona'	'Bartigon'	'William Pitt'
'Kees Nelis'			

Long-lived Tulips

Tom Powell of the *Avant Gardener* lists the following bulbs for deep planting. If the soil is properly prepared to a depth of 18 inches and the bulbs planted 10 to 12 inches deep, they will blossom for five years or more.

'Anton Mauve'
'Arethusa'
'Clara Butt'
'Dom Pedro'
'Fantasy'
'Faust'
'Fiancee'
'Indian Chief'
'Inglescombe Yellow'
'Jeanne Desor'
'Kathleen Parlow'
'King George V'
'Louis IV'
'Mayflower'
'Martha'
'Monica'
'Persimmon'
'Picotee'
'Prince of Wales'
'Rev. H. Ewbank'
'Zwanenburg'

Books for Further Reading

Brooklyn Botanic Garden, *Handbook on Bulbs.* 1959

Crockett, J. U., *Bulbs.* Time-Life, 1971

Earle, Alice Morse, *Old Time Gardens.* Macmillan, 1911.

Genders, Roy, *A Complete Handbook of Bulbs, Corms and Tubers.* Bobbs-Merrill Co., Inc., 1973.

Hedrick, U. P., *A History of Horticulture in America to 1860.* Oxford University Press, 1950.

Kasperski, Victoria, *How to Make Cut Flowers Last.* Barrows, 1956.

Miles, Bebe, *The Wonderful World of Bulbs.* D. Van Nostrand Company, Inc., 1959.

Reynolds, M., and Meachem, W. L., *The Garden Bulbs of Spring.* Funk & Wagnalls, 1967.

Rockwell, F. F., and Grayson, Esther, *The Complete Book of Bulbs,* revised and edited by Marjorie J. Dietz. J. B. Lippincott Company, 1977.

Illustration Credits